Praise for *Tenacity*

"Keith is a wonderful storyteller! He made me feel like I was right there with him in Nepal on his adventure. This is such a fun read for anyone on the path of self-discovery."

—Traci Brown
Speaker and Body Language Expert
Author of *How to Detect Lies, Fraud and Identity Theft*
www.tracibrown.com

"Keith is one of the most adventurous and inquisitive people I know! His story of *Tenacity* is significant in that it shows how to see your life as a journey of experiences—good and bad—which allow you to evolve and grow."

—Connie M. Warden…The Well-Being Warrior
Author of *SELF – LEADERSHIPPING:*
Pursuing Your Full Potential Using Curiosity, Courage & Consistency
www.conniewarden.com

"*Tenacity* is a wonderful mix of adventure, personal empowerment, and motivation all wrapped up in journey through Nepal. Keith's "TRIP System" (Tenacity, Resilience, Imagination and Purpose) became real to him while lost in the Himalayas. A wonderful read!"

—Marlene Bizub, PhD.
Author of *Contentious Custody: Is It Really in the Best Interest of Your Children?* www.marlenebizub.com

"Keith's new book, *Tenacity*, is an entertaining adventure in self-discovery. Sometimes it takes getting lost to find ourselves."

—Orvel Ray Wilson
Co-author of the *Guerrilla Marketing* series.
www.GuerrillaGroup.com

TENACITY

AN ADVENTURE MEMOIR

TENACITY

You Don't Have to Get Lost in Nepal to Find Yourself, But It Helps!

Keith Renninson

Shellhouse
Press

Tenacity: You Don't Have to Get Lost in Nepal to Find Yourself, But It Helps!

Published by Shellhouse Press.

Keith Renninson
Phone: 303-973-1643 Email: keith@keithrenninson.com
www.keithrenninson.com

ISBN: 978-0-692-75787-1

Editor: Tyler Tichelaar/Superior Book Productions
Additional editing: Orvel Ray Wilson
Additional editing: Vicki Tosher
Proofreader: Larry Alexander/Superior Book Productions
Cover Design: Andrea Costantine
All Photographs: Keith Renninson
Interior Book Design: Andrea Costantine
Author Photo: Stephanie Pomponio

Every attempt has been made to properly source all quotes.
Printed in the United States of America
First Edition 2 4 6 8 10 12

To my parents, Ed and Clara Renninson
And my son Michael,
With Love and Gratitude

"Everything You Desire is Just Outside Your Comfort Zone"

CONTENTS

NOTE FROM THE AUTHOR

We all have wonderful experiences in life that we feel are worthy of sharing, *Tenacity* is that story for me. Being in my late '40's at the time I traveled to Nepal, I was at a crossroads in life and knew I needed to evaluate where to go next.

If you find yourself in your mid-life crisis, don't despair, it's just a time to look deeply at your life and make changes that will be positive and growth oriented. Stay on course, make adjustments as necessary and don't lose faith.

Some names in my story have been changed. And the experiences I write about are how I remember them. If there are any mistakes, please know that they are not intentional. My experiences are based on my 25+ year memory and the notes in my journal.

I wish you well in your journey and hope that you open the door to self-discovery when it knocks; you will be glad you did.

When in doubt, take a TRIP!

Keith

ACKNOWLEDGMENTS

Even though this book has been a labor of love, it took the gentle prodding of a lot of family and friends to keep me on track. No more was this evident than from the support and encouragement of my parents, Ed and Clara. Their love and confidence in me were an ever-present force that allowed me to know I was on the right track and to continue when I thought of quitting. Unfortunately, my Mom passed away before it was published, but I'm sure she would be proud of the result. My son, Michael, also gave me his thoughtful and helpful feedback and support as I did my final edits.

A small band of close friends also kept asking how I was doing and thus laid just enough of a guilt trip on me to keep me moving the project forward. Among those were Patty Cathey, Jeff Blatt, Stan Kropewnicki, Connie Warden, Doreen Cumberford, Marlene Moser Bizub, COBRAS Cycling Members, Orvel Ray Wilson, Norma Brown, Betty Schwab, Traci Brown and Keith Horowitz.

To each of these people, I wish to express my gratitude for their encouragement over the years it took me to write & re-write *Tenacity,* and for understanding the emotional peaks and valleys that a writer must endure while writing and editing.

INTRODUCTION

The age-old statement, "Be careful what you ask for because you might just get it," certainly holds true for me. After my first trip to Asia in 1970, compliments of the U.S. Army, I always wished to visit other countries there. That day came in 1992, when a friend, Denise, and I journeyed to Nepal for three weeks of trekking in the Himalayas. Having grown up in Colorado, I thought Nepal seemed very similar because the plains turn into the foothills of a mountain range and set the stage for high peaks, glaciers, and spectacular scenery. Nepal is also a place of mystical tranquility; it is steeped in spirituality, which was perfect at the time.

In 1995, it was time to return to Nepal, but this time, I chose to travel alone. It had been one of those magical years, and I didn't want it to end. I had self-published my first book, *The Pain and Joy of Love*, and it had rolled off the press just two weeks before my trek.

But more importantly, I had discovered my metaphysical self. It had been a quest that had spanned the previous five years. I had just hit my stride in self-examination and the wonderful spiritual discoveries that come with that path. I had begun to recognize how blessed my life was and the personal powers I had been given.

Those powers included one that was particularly strong, my "*knowing*." We all experience it; some people call it intuition. It comes from meditation and a feeling of connectedness with God, the universe, and my soul. This internal power enhanced my tenacity, resilience, imagination and purpose in life.

Arriving in Bangkok, the news was all about severe rains in Kathmandu and heavy snow near Everest. Since the goal was to trek to Everest Base Camp, this was distressing information.

The next day, at the Kathmandu airport, numerous helicopters were landing just a few hundred yards away. The ground crews were unloading black body bags onto the tarmac; the remains of trekkers killed in avalanches. I knew then that my plans were going to change.

I used the next three days to redesign the trek, exchange my permits for a new destination, make alternate flight arrangements, and figure out what I would leave behind in Kathmandu and what I would carry.

I settled on a mountain named Kanchenjunga in the northeast region of Nepal. It was a more lawless area of the country, and my travel advisor in Kathmandu wasn't very excited by my choice. My *knowing*, however, told me to go. My determination made it happen.

I asked for adventure, to be my own Indiana Jones, and as the days unfolded, I got exactly what I asked for. At no time was that more evident than on the fourth day of my trip, and the first day of the trek near Kanchenjunga. I got lost. Fortunately, that was just the beginning.

Writing this memoir was a catharsis of sorts for me as I remembered many memories while I was lost. Those memories helped me find myself and revealed strengths that I knew I had but had suppressed. It took a long time to write and publish this book as I wasn't sure I wanted to share my ups and downs from life. But writing them in this manner also helped me grow again. Growth in life comes in spurts between everything else.

It was during this time in Nepal that my keynote and workshop was formulating in my mind although the words changed over time until I settled on: ***"TRIP: Tenacity, Resilience, Imagination and Purpose"***. These four words were the essence of what I learned about myself and life in general. I hope through my stories here you find your way to them as well.

PART ONE

"I LOVE YOU"

The day I left Denver, a blizzard was settling in the area, and it had made getting to the new airport difficult. DIA (Denver International Airport) is about forty miles from home, and the roads were treacherous. My friend Sandy drove through the storm in early morning darkness, and we were late. As I rushed to the international flight desk, I could hear the "last call" for my 5:30 a.m. flight being announced.

"I can call the gate and have the plane held for you, but I can't get your luggage on this flight. I will put it on the next flight; where do you want it checked through to?" asked the attendant hurriedly.

"Oh, great; you mean I could arrive halfway around the world and not have any underwear?"

"Why, yes, I guess that is a real possibility," she said apprehensively.

"Well, that's life in the slow lane," I said, laughing. "Please check it through to Bangkok."

"It's so nice of you to have a sense of humor about it; most people would be very angry with me over this."

"It's not your fault that I'm late, and it's snowing. All I can do is know that all will turn out okay and keep on truckin'."

"Well, I'll do my best, but for now, you need to hurry, since I can only hold the plane for a short time. Good luck and have a great time," the attendant hollered as I ran down the concourse.

The door closed right after I boarded, and the plane taxied to the de-icing station. I found my seat and settled in. I know I should have felt at least some anxiety over this inauspicious start, but instead, there was an overwhelming sense of wonder and excitement. A great thing about *knowing* is when it's real, you know.

In Bangkok, I inquired after my luggage. The attendant said it had not yet arrived, but she would have it checked through to Kathmandu. Luckily, my carry-on bag contained toiletries and a change of underwear.

The eighteen-hour flight to Bangkok was exhausting, so I checked into the in-airport hotel and slept like a baby. Arriving in Kathmandu the next day around noon, I entered the baggage claim area, and there, waiting for me, were all of my pieces of luggage. All I could do was laugh and be grateful for good fortune.

I had brought along a lot of photographic equipment, clothing, and food. It weighed too much, about fifty-five pounds, but then I never packed light. Believe me, I do now.

My close friend and travel agent, Shyam "Sam" Shrestha, also owned The Mt. Everest Restaurant in Denver. He also owned a home in Kathmandu, and I was to stay there with his brother, Lava.

Exiting customs, I was pleased to see Lava holding a sign with my name. Over the next three days, he was a great help in obtaining my trekking permits and documents. He was shy and didn't speak much English, but we made out just fine.

In the week prior, Nepal had suffered a very unusual storm that had dumped a lot of rain on the lower elevations near Kathmandu and more than six feet of snow in the mountains.

This was the prime trekking season because the weather was usually mild. However, this year no trekkers were being allowed in many regions because of the high number of deaths from avalanches.

I was outfitted for a high, cold trek, but now I was relegated to a much different excursion in the northeastern corner of Nepal known as Kanchenjunga. Named after the second highest mountain in Nepal at 28,169 feet. I obtained the necessary permits and left the next day.

After a two-hour flight past Mt. Everest in a rickety single-engine, eight-passenger plane, I landed in Bhaktupur. I was to spend the night with Suba, a relative of my travel advisors in the States, Sam and Shenti Shrestha. Suba was a thoroughly delightful man, who worked as a customs officer at the Nepal-India border.

The next day I started a two-day bus trip to my ultimate destination Cavalli, along the way we stopped to spend the night in the town of Illam. It seemed surprisingly clean. Most of Nepal feels overwhelmingly poverty-stricken and with that comes unsanitary and dirty conditions. You can sense that the people know their plight, but they don't have the resources to improve it. This town seemed to have a greater sense of civic pride and better cash flow. The modern local industry, growing tea, obviously had helped raise the standard of living. From the bus window, the tea gardens stretched in every direction. The air was sweet and clean, and you could see for miles up the valleys.

I was feeling a wonderful sense of adventure on my second day in Nepal. My first trip here three years earlier had been with a friend, and although I felt some of the same delight, it wasn't the same.

Being alone in a Third World country without speaking much of the language, heightened my awareness.

The previous six years for me had been difficult emotionally and financially. I had suffered through a divorce, a downturn in business, the loss of a subsequent girlfriend, and I had been in a general funk. I desperately needed this vacation.

It was 1:30 p.m. when I stepped off the bus, offloaded my pack, and started to look for a place to spend the night. I was hungry and tired, but the chance to wander about a new town and take some pictures beckoned to me. Much to my delight, I found a nice hotel adjacent to the parking lot. The hotel clerk had a good sense of humor; I haggled with him for a few pleasant moments, and then he escorted me to my room. I had come to enjoy the give and take of barter, and some of the natives were more fun than others. I love to tease and play with people no matter where I am, and here the people liked it too. Once settled in my room, I grabbed my camera, padlocked my room door, and went out exploring.

I wandered for over an hour without seeing another trekker, and I was getting the impression that I was the only one in town. The lack of tourists made me stand out, and the townsfolk seemed quite amused by my presence. Word seemed to spread quite rapidly; soon many villagers had gathered in front of the small restaurant where I had some noodles. Some would point and laugh while others would wave to me, talking among themselves and having great fun. On my first trip, it had taken a while to get used to this kind of attention. It's like being a celebrity, which obviously has its ups and downs. It is worth noting that the Nepalese people (or Nepalis) openly express their curiosity and playfulness, which I found very refreshing. I had come to enjoy the attention, plus it gave me the opportunity for some great pictures.

Around 3:00 p.m., I tired of walking and needed a nap, so I returned to my hotel room and lay down. I had just dropped off to sleep when a small knock on my door woke me. At first, I thought

I'd been dreaming, but the gentle knock sounded again. "Who could that possibly be?" I mumbled to myself. As I slowly opened the door, I saw the young hotel clerk and a small Nepalese man who looked to be about thirty years old.

"Namaste. Suba call me; eh, you Keef?" said the little man in a soft, quiet, and apprehensive voice. His accent was very thick, and his English was brand new. As hard to understand as he was, the name Suba came through clearly. This young man's name was Rajenda.

Suba had contacted Rajenda to make sure I was okay and to look out for me. He had been to all the hotels, teahouses, and guest-rooms trying to find me. Since hotels here don't use registers, he had to spend several hours asking around for my whereabouts. I had left a trail of townspeople I had photographed and spoken to all afternoon, so he just followed the stories of the stranger who was in town.

Rajenda was here to give me a tour of Illam. I was tired and really didn't want to go, but he was so kind and insistent that I gave in. I retrieved my camera and a bottle of water, locked the door, and we left. He didn't talk much as I followed him into the tea gardens. He would just point to buildings or the view of the valley, smile, and nod to me. I would smile and nod back.

At first, walking through the tea gardens was like taking any other stroll. The late afternoon temperature was in the low seventies, and the visibility was excellent. The brilliance of the sun warmed my face, while the cool air kept me comfortable. Everywhere I looked, the rich color of green surrounded me. There were very few trees, but plenty of beautifully groomed, waist-high tea plants. Birds greeted me with their chirping, and you could hear the occasional dog barking. Off in the distance, columns of smoke rose from the kitchens of the small homes that dotted the hillsides as people prepared their evening meals.

When we first started out, I had hoped this tour wouldn't take too long. I had risen early to catch my bus. As we walked along, I took pictures of Rajenda and the gardens. The mountains weren't steep as much as they were rolling. Barefoot workers carrying tea leaves in large cloth bags to the processing sheds in the town had made the moist, dark-brown dirt path smooth and even.

IT WAS DURING THIS TIME OF SELF-EXAMINATION THAT I DEVELOPED AN INTENSE DESIRE TO KNOW MORE ABOUT OUR HUMAN EXISTENCE. MANY QUESTIONS BEGAN SURFACING THAT I COULDN'T ANSWER BUT LONGED TO SOLVE. I CALLED THEM MY "WHAT IF" QUESTIONS. WHAT IF THE PROBABILITY OF LIMITLESS CREATIVITY AND ENERGY ACTUALLY EXISTS? WHAT IF I COULD LIVE SO EXQUISITELY IN THE MOMENT OF A PURE STATE OF NO PAST AND NO FUTURE THAT REGRET AND WORRY DISAPPEARED? WHAT IF I COULD HARNESS THE ENERGY OF "BEING" AND PUT IT TO WORK ESTABLISHING A LINK BETWEEN MY MIND/SOUL AND THE INFINITE RESOURCES OF THE UNIVERSAL KNOWLEDGE? IF I COULD SIDESTEP THE MUNDANE AND ONLY SEE THE MAGNIFICENT POTENTIAL IN EVERY MOMENT, WHAT COULD I ACCOMPLISH? WHAT IF I COULD BE MENTALLY DISCIPLINED ENOUGH TO SEIZE THAT POWER—THEN WHAT PHENOMENA WOULD OCCUR? WOULD THE QUANTUM THEORIES OF PROBABILITY AND UNCERTAINTY ALLOW THE DIVERSITY OF CREATIVE THOUGHT TO FLOW

TO ME AND THROUGH ME? WHAT IF I COULD CAPTURE THE UNIVERSAL KNOWLEDGE FOR A SPECIFIC, LIMITED PERIOD OF TIME? WHAT THEN WOULD I LEARN, AND COULD I PROCESS IT? ISN'T IT POSSIBLE TO FIND A WAY TO ACCOMPLISH THESE THINGS? AS A HUMAN WITH LIMITATIONS, IS IT POSSIBLE? OR DO I HAVE ONLY SELF-IMPOSED LIMITATIONS? IN THE END, WILL I DISCOVER THAT I AM LIMITLESS, BUT AS A HUMAN, I CAN ONLY SEE THE BOUNDARIES I'VE CREATED?

WHAT IF I COULD USE THE ENERGY OBTAINED FROM THE ELIMINATION OF REPETITIVE PAST AND FUTURE THINKING TO SLEEP LESS? COULD THE ADDITIONAL HOURS GAINED FROM NOT SLEEPING BE UTILIZED FOR MORE CREATIVE THOUGHT, OR WOULD INSUFFICIENT REST HINDER IT?

WOULD THE CREATIVE QUESTS GET LOST IN THE PRODUCTION THAT WOULD ULTIMATELY FOLLOW? IF I COULD MANIFEST A LIFESTYLE DEVOTED TO CREATIVITY, WOULD I BE ABLE TO MAINTAIN IT? AND FINALLY, IF I COULD FOLLOW MY HEART AND SOUL'S PATH COMPLETELY, WHAT WOULD IT LOOK LIKE?

Walking along slowly, feeling calm and comfortable, letting my mind be at peace, connected to God, and enjoying the freedom of my trip, I was truly living in the moment. The inner peace that permeated my whole being was so strong that I couldn't help but be aware of it. Suddenly, while looking at the ground in front of me, I saw, scribbled in the dirt, the words "I love you." I stopped and stared, not believing what I was seeing. Here I was fifty-some miles deep into Nepal where very few people spoke English, let alone knew how to write it, yet the love and peace I had been feeling was expressed back to me by someone having the same experience. I pointed to the words and asked Rajenda if he knew what they meant; he said he didn't know how to read English, smiled, and beckoned me to follow in another direction. Knowing that no one would believe me, I took a picture of the words. My recent teachings told me always to look upon these occurrences with a sense of awe and wonder; there was no other way I could reflect on this one. I found it very special, and I was thankful to whoever had placed the words there.

I had never been much of a reader or someone who studied much of anything with passion. Maybe it was due to the changes in my life in recent years, but my reading of philosophy and metaphysics had acquired an urgency and purpose. Many books suddenly appeared before me through friends and relatives that lighted a fire of curiosity in my soul. Examples include: *Think and Grow Rich* by Napoleon Hill, *Conversations with God* by Neale Donald Walsh, *Way of the Peaceful Warrior* by Dan Millman, *Jonathan Livingston Seagull* by Richard Bach, and *Fingerprints of the Gods* by Graham Hancock. I became an avid reader. From many of those books and articles, I began watching my awareness and spirituality for clues to living a better life. Even the smallest occurrence didn't get past me without some examination. "I love you" was one of the occurrences that held meaning for me and somehow made me feel closer to God and the Universe.

As I viewed it, my life simply would be one of being healthy, happy, and wise, living a life filled with love, prosperity, and creativity. I felt that I was almost there, and I hoped this trek would open the door to the rest. As these thoughts ran through my mind, I followed Rajenda through the quiet tea gardens on a warm, sunny afternoon.

Illam was indeed a fortunate town. The Japanese had adopted the city and invested many hundreds of thousands of yen into a water purification system. They had gone high up into the Himalayas to run underground pipes that fed water down to Illam. Then, they had built a modern plant to make the water the most drinkable and safe in all of Nepal. This water, coupled with a very prosperous tea business, made the local economy extremely stable. It even showed in Rajenda; he was healthy, well-dressed, and filled with pride for his town.

After walking around the tea gardens and the water plant, Rajenda took me to a compound of four buildings with well-manicured grounds and trees. Inside one building were four men who also knew Suba. They offered me a cup of chai and a cookie. None of them spoke English any better than my guide, but for an hour they tried to make me feel comfortable. They worked as accountants for the Nepali government at this facility. Tax collecting is nearly as old as the Himalayas, and so was their recording system. On their large, old, wooden desks were enormous ledgers in which they would record the taxes paid by various people and businesses in the area. It looked like an American Old West assay office with books of claims. The ledger books were two feet square and four inches thick, and everything was recorded by hand in ink.

Along with the water plant, the Japanese had built an updated electrical system through an ingenious hydroelectric plant. This gave the citizens of Illam better than average conditions in which to do their work. The lighting wasn't great for these men by American standards, but it was the best I'd seen in Nepal by far.

I finished my tea and then asked if I could take the men's picture on the front steps. They all seemed eager to participate and smiled on cue. They waved, as Rajenda and another man escorted me back to my hotel.

Walking through the village, the two men seemed to revel in the ability to elevate themselves in the community by being with someone new and different. They walked slowly and waved to many friends, making small comments. I found the notoriety somewhat humorous but fun. Once we said our goodbyes, and I was back in my room, I was glad to eat one of my Clif bars and read my book.

As I fell asleep in Illam, I wondered whether my trip was as blessed as I felt, or whether I was just behaving foolishly. My thoughts strayed to my stay with Suba the night before which hadn't been without serious insight into local violence.

Suba was a thoroughly delightful man, who worked as a customs officer at the Nepal-India border. Like border towns in many countries, it was very unsafe. In the middle of the night, I was awakened by the screams of a man outside Suba's home. I hurriedly put on my pants and sandals and ran outside to see what was going on. Suba and two other men were standing over the body of a man who had been stabbed. In the dim light of their flashlights, I could see blood running from his back into the dust of the dirt street.

"Suba, what happened?" I asked.

"This man had been spending a lot of money in a bar and was attacked by someone who wanted his money," he replied sadly.

"Can I be of any help?"

"No. My men here will take care of it. You can go back to bed."

Suba's wife had warned me earlier in the evening of the dangerous territory I was in and that it was not safe to travel alone. She tried to get me to change my travel plans, but I couldn't change them again. It left me with an eerie feeling, and yet I was so calm otherwise.

CAVALLI

Each day dawned with renewed excitement as my adventure continued. I awoke at 6:00 a.m. and hurried down to the ticket shack in the bus station parking lot. The two men in charge were drinking the dark black tea known as chai and smoking foul-smelling Indian cigarettes. On the counter sat an old-fashioned kerosene lantern, which rendered the only light in the still darkened wooden hut. They looked at me warily, but took my money when I told them I wished to continue to Cavalli. I tried to arrange to sit in the same front first-class seat I had coming from Karkarvita/Bhaktupur bus stop the day before. When I boarded, I discovered that a prominent person from Illam had beaten me to it and I was told to sit in the first row behind the closed off first-class section … behind the chain link fence. Later in the day, this proved to be a very interesting spot.

In the early morning light, I crossed the dirt parking lot and entered a cafe for chai and chapati. I had learned on my first trip to Nepal that breakfast was going to be my favorite meal. The chai was served several ways, straight black or as a milk-tea mixed with cinnamon and sometimes pepper. Chapati is a wheat flatbread that looks like a fat tortilla. It is generally served with honey or mandarin orange jam. At some teahouses, you could also get old-fashioned porridge along with the chapati and chai, which made me very happy.

The cafe owner quietly sat smoking a cigarette and drinking tea while an employee busied himself cleaning the counter and sweeping, all the while looking nervously at his employer, who largely ignored him.

The cook brought my chai in a small glass on a tin tray. It was steaming in the cool morning air, too hot to hold, so I placed it on the arm of my wooden chair. I have always hated my lack of tolerance to hold hot objects with my fingers.

Illam was a quiet town in these early morning hours, the only people out were children and shopkeepers. After breakfast, I played with a group of small children who had gathered to watch me shooting photos. They would giggle, I would take their picture, and then they would laugh some more. The sound of children giggling in the morning is always pleasant to me. I love playing with little kids; they are so willing to play and tease. It is too bad we tend to lose that quality when we become adults.

The sun was just coming up when the bus driver started the noisy engine, which was a signal for the passengers to begin boarding. The driver then informed me that I now had to sit in the seat just behind the steps entering the bus on its left side. Oddly, the drivers sit on the right in Nepalese buses, and you enter on the left.

There is a wire mesh screen that separates six first-class seats from the rest of the coach.

I was seated next to a schoolteacher from Kathmandu who spoke very good English. He was nice, but a shade distant, a trait I found to be common among the educated class in Nepal. Nevertheless, we talked a lot and enjoyed each other as the day wore on.

As had been the mode of operation the previous day, we would drive fast over rough roads and pick up passengers along the way. The temperature dropped in the overcast mountains as we climbed higher and higher. It was then that I noticed everyone had warm winter coats, hats, and gloves. If the bus had a heater, I couldn't feel it.

Around 10:00 a.m., the driver pulled the bus over to the side of the road and stopped. The driver's assistant announced something in Nepalese, and everyone rose and hurriedly exited the bus. I looked at my teacher friend and asked curiously, "What's going on?"

"It's time to use the toilet."

I exited the bus and looked around for some structure housing toilets; instead, I saw everyone, men and women, standing or squatting near the side of the road, urinating or defecating. Since I needed to urinate also, the timing was right. I felt a little uncomfortable since most of the passengers watched to see whether I would follow their custom or act differently. When they saw me going also, they seemed to be pleased.

During my first trip, I learned as travelers everywhere do, how to say, "Hello," "Thank you," "Where's the toilet?" etc. Well, "Namaste," pronounced nam-es-taa, is similar to "Aloha," translating to "Hello" and "Goodbye." Upon returning home, a friend shared with me this word's ancient Sanskrit meaning: "My world is better with you in it." Since then, I have felt that this was a very special greeting.

I got a lot more smiles and namastes as people reentered the bus. Suddenly, there was a hum of conversation and activity. The woman to my right was breastfeeding her baby while gossiping with the lady seated next to her. Children cried and played, and men read newspapers while others sat and looked out their windows—a pretty normal bus ride the world over.

Some very beautiful scenery passed by my window for the next two hours. Deep valleys full of lush vegetation, and distant, high, majestic peaks beckoned to me with previews of days to come. The road turned to a rough dirt surface around 11:00 a.m. The huge "Tata" bus, the name of the manufacturer, would rock slowly from side to side as the driver negotiated the potholes and ruts made by the rushing streams that we crossed.

Shortly after noon, the bus stopped in front of what looked like an Old West stagecoach stop. A couple of stone buildings built on the side of a steep slope faced an incredible view of the Himalayas. Lunch was included with your ticket; unfortunately, it was dahl bhat—the staple food item for two meals per day for most of Nepal—and for which I had never acquired the taste. Made of lentils and broth, it is poured over white rice. Other people I know dearly love it, but I have to add salt, pepper, and any available hot sauce to bring it to my liking. The Nepalese eat it by using the fingers of the right hand. Eating with the right hand is traditional in Asia since the people cleanse themselves with the left. My newly acquired friend said he would be honored if I would allow him to buy me lunch. He said that the noodles and beer would be much more to my liking. I accepted his offer and did indeed enjoy the hot broth and noodles. Afterward, the bus driver and his mechanic busied themselves checking the bus for needed repairs, while the passengers smoked and talked to each other. The day was finally becoming a little warmer, so I removed my jacket.

The fluffy clouds rolled by quickly in the obvious jet stream flowing off the Himalayas. The sky was a rich deep blue and offset the green of the paradise below. After a short while, we re-boarded the bus and flew down the dirt road, bouncing along like characters in a cartoon.

A couple of hours later, we arrived at Phadim, and I lost my traveling companion to his destination. Phadim was supposed to be a major regional town, but it was very dirty and poor. We took on additional passengers, and instantly, the bus was over capacity. Many people carried sacks of grain, which they would lay in the aisle and then stand on.

As we left Phadim, we went down a steep incline, crossed a wooden plank bridge that I was sure would collapse under the weight of the bus, and started up the other side, which was equally steep and narrow. The transmission of the bus groaned at the steepness of the road and the tremendous weight it was now carrying. The temperature had risen to the upper seventies, so with the heat and the number of people on the bus, I was becoming claustrophobic.

One thing was also becoming very noticeable; the odor on the bus had taken a turn for the worse. With the occasional pig, bags of grain, vegetables, and people, there was a plethora of odors. A woman had entered the bus and was standing next to my right shoulder on a sack of rice. She was carrying a chicken under her right arm and holding on to a hand strap from the ceiling with her left. Unfortunately, she was rather overweight and filled the aisle. As the bus would turn right, she would press her large, left breast into my shoulder and face and then smile at me with a toothless grin. There was nowhere for me to go, and my claustrophobia was getting worse.

Earlier in the day, I had noticed that outside the window to my left, the driver's mechanic would use a ladder attached to the bus to carry luggage or other cargo onto the roof. Finally, when I could stand it no more, I told the man seated to my left that I was going out the window. He looked at me with a startled expression, because the bus was going about 35-40 mph. I stood up and squeezed myself through the window, which wasn't easy with my fanny pack, a water bottle on my belt, and my camera around my neck. I pulled myself up and out of the bus using the ladder rungs and climbed onto the roof. It was dusty, but I could breathe. What a relief!

As I looked for a place to sit among the cargo, four rather tough-looking young men in their early twenties surveyed me. They watched me in amazement, laughing and talking very fast and pointing at me. It was difficult to stand up with the bus bouncing and turning, so I quickly sat down before I lost my balance. There was a spot next to the cargo that I could back up against to sit, so I hurriedly moved there. To my right was a small railing that ran around the bus about six inches above the roof. Ropes securing the cargo were tied to it to keep the cargo from sliding off. To my left was a twenty-four-year-old Nepali with a big smile and lots of black hair. He knew a few words of English, so he asked me where I was from and where I was going. He then shared my answers with his friends.

A little later, he and his friends sang a song together and tried to teach me the words. It was fun, and we all laughed a lot. As the afternoon wore on, we tired of the amusement we found in each other, and everyone became quiet. They must have accepted me because as we sat facing the rear of the bus, watching the scenery go by, the young man took my left arm and placed it around him. He then laid his head on my chest and went to sleep. The act moved me, to say the least. In Nepal, as in many other parts of the world, men will hold hands or walk arm-in-arm as nothing more than a sign of friendship. It is only in the Western world that people look upon this behavior with prejudice.

I must have dozed off also for a short while. I was tired from the day's activities and needed the nap. You learn to sleep in the strangest places when you are on the road traveling like this.

Sometime later, something hard was jabbing into my stomach rudely awakened me. The sun was directly behind the individual standing above me, and at first, I couldn't see who it was. I sat up abruptly, frightened and angry, only to discover that it was a Gurkha, a Nepalese soldier, pushing a large rifle barrel into my side and shouting at me. The boy next to me said the soldier wanted us to return to the seats in the bus.

I was relieved that he didn't want to see my trekking permit, I smiled and hurried to my seat below. The boy sat next to me and explained that there are Gurkha checkpoints along the road to stop smuggling and catch robbers. By now, I was a good thirty miles beyond where my permit allowed me to go, so phew, I felt lucky.

IT'S A FUNNY THING ABOUT INTUITION OR KNOWING, AS I CALL IT; IF YOU HAVE ALLOWED YOURSELF TO RECOGNIZE IT WHEN IT OCCURS, THERE IS NO OTHER EXPLANATION FOR THE SITUATION BEFORE YOU. YOU REALLY HAVE NO CHOICE; WELL, I SUPPOSE YOU DO, BUT WHY NOT FOLLOW THE GUIDANCE BEING OFFERED BY A HIGHER POWER? SOME WOULD SAY THAT THEY WOULD FIND SUCH GUIDANCE DIFFICULT TO FOLLOW SINCE THEY HAVE NO PROOF OF ITS EXISTENCE OR WHETHER IT'S GOOD ADVICE TO BEGIN WITH. IT ALL BOILS DOWN TO FAITH AND TRUST. IF YOU DON'T HAVE EITHER, YOU WON'T GET PAST YOUR OWN EGO LONG ENOUGH TO LET THE GUIDANCE LEAD YOU. IT HAS TAKEN ME A LONG TIME TO COME TO AN UNDERSTANDING OF THIS CONCEPT, BUT NOW I RELY ON IT DAILY.

Trekking and climbing permits are part of the gross national product in Nepal. They are issued at varying rates. Shorter distances in trekking and higher mountains in climbing havprices commensurate with the length of the trek in time or distance or height of the mountain you climb. Some are cheap at $5.00. Others are over

$700.00 plus an additional cost per day beyond that. With my limited time, I wasn't sure how close to Kanchenjunga I would get, so I purchased a permit that would get me far enough that I didn't think anyone would care if I went a little beyond its boundary.

Throughout the trek, every time I faced some sort of sticky situation, a *knowing* deep down inside told me I was safe and to remain calm.

The bus had almost emptied as the afternoon had progressed, so I wasn't as claustrophobic. The high, narrow road had gotten much rougher if that were possible. The steepness of the mountain terrain had also increased. Whenever we would meet another bus or Tata truck, both vehicles would stop, and one would back up to a semi-wide spot where the buses would jockey past each other. Maximum speed had dropped to 20 to 25 mph because of the ruts and the sheer drop off into valley thousands of feet below.

The Tata buses are incredible. They are extremely tough and take a lot of abuse, although I noticed the driver and his mechanic checking the suspension and tires every time we stopped. This knowledge made me feel secure and insecure at the same time. Because of the heavy loads that the buses carry in humans and cargo, they are heavily sprung and sit high off the ground, much like some of the four-wheel drive recreational vehicles at home. This causes them to rock back and forth when the bus bounces over ruts or potholes. Whenever the driver would come up to a blind corner, he would lay on his horn loudly and continue at the same speed around the corner. The drivers rarely slowed down, which seemed reckless and curious to me because of the people's inherently religious nature here. They held life so dear, and yet they drove like maniacs.

Several children who spoke very good English boarded the bus on the way to Cavalli, and we had a good time talking. They had many questions and were eager to try out their second language. I exchanged addresses with several of them, wondering whether I would ever hear from them. I suppose they were thinking the same thing, and unfortunately, we never did.

It started getting dark, and I wasn't sure whether my pack was with me. I hadn't been able to spot it when I was riding on the roof. When you are alone, you sometimes tend to worry about things over which you have no control.

The road became very rutted, and our speed dropped even further as we descended into a deep valley. At times, the angle of descent seemed so severe that I found myself holding on to the railing in front of me to keep from sliding off my seat.

Funny thing about darkness and our imaginations, they make for a lethal combination. Why is it that the moment control is gone, fear and imagination take over? That little voice that resides in the back of our minds suddenly becomes a very large and noisy child screaming to take charge and lead us into a sweaty state of panic. My little voice was about to start screaming, and I knew it.

We picked up some additional passengers, and one man was incensed that I was an American, alone, and didn't speak much Nepalese. A Maoist, he kept pointing at me and talking about me to the other passengers in the front cabin in a nasty tone of voice. As this uncomfortable situation continued, I started asking myself the expected questions: *Am I on the right bus? Should I have transferred at one of the previous stops? Is my gear safe and on the bus? Will I be able to find a place to stay in Cavalli when we get there?* Finally, *what the hell am I doing out here, by myself, to begin with?*

I swear that God and the Universe are constantly watching over me because a rescue was on the way. It came as a voice out of the chilly darkness from the seat behind me.

As the bus approached Cavalli, a young Nepali man sitting behind me reached out to me, telling me he was in the Nepalese army and was heading home on leave. In a soft reassuring tone, he told me we were close to the end of our journey, and if I walked to the building next to the bus when it stopped, I would find food and a room for the night.

He said to walk quickly because many of the passengers would be going to the same place. I appreciated my friend in the dark, and sure enough, his directions proved to be sincere and accurate. As I stood, all the passengers stood and formed a barrier between the angry Maoist and me. I moved quickly to get away from him.

My pack was handed down to me almost at the same moment as I exited the bus by the boy from the roof, and I walked quickly to the teahouse. A smelly diesel generator was running to the side of the building, and the glare of several raw 60-watt lightbulbs gave the blackened night eerie shadows. Children from the bus and the local families ran among the passengers, playing and laughing. Being very tired and running on little food and sleep, the whole scene was like a distorted dream.

I approached the building where a tall woman at an outdoor counter negotiated with me for a room and a meal. Both came to only forty rupees. That's about twenty cents in American currency. As it turned out, the woman was the owner's wife. She looked more Indian than Nepali, very tall, slender, and dark-skinned. Using a flashlight, she led me back through a dark hallway and through the kitchen that was lit by the cooking fire. The smoke was thick, and it stung my lungs and eyes., I immediately felt sorry for the young girls working there.

We went up a wooden ladder to the second floor and back toward the front of the building. I followed her, the floor creaking beneath me, but in the dim light, it was difficult. Along the way in the large room there were numerous cots with a blanket thrown over each of them. Some people had already lain down for the night, while others were sitting, talking and smoking awful-smelling Asian cigarettes.

We came to a door, which she opened. Inside were two cots about six feet long and three feet wide. The room was only seven by seven, leaving a foot between the cots. A window on one side looked out on the area where the bus was parked. The other three walls were wooden and bare. As we stood there together, we had to stoop slightly because the ceiling was so low. I told her I would take the room and paid her, at which point she exited, closing the door behind her.

I got out my flashlight, sat on one of the cots, and put my gear on the other. Oddly, I felt safe in a room that I could lock and where I could be alone—as if I weren't already as alone as I could get. I pulled out the baby wipes I had brought along, cleaned my face and hands, and rested for a few moments, letting the needed serenity sink in. Then I locked the room with my padlock and went back downstairs for some dahl baht and a beer. I'm not much of a beer drinker, but I feared how clean the bottled water might be.

Several other people were eating in the small room set aside as a restaurant. Luckily, there was no sign of the angry man from the bus. I sat at one of the six wooden, picnic-style tables and benches that filled the room. The noise of the arriving passengers had all but died down, and only the steady hum of the generator filled the air. I could smell food being prepared in the dark, grimy kitchen and some incense burning next to a Hindu altar in one corner. The air was cool, but it seemed dense with humidity.

As I sat and waited for my dinner, I watched the owner's wife. She was probably 5' 10" and had striking features. She wore a typical bandana, a white, short-sleeve blouse, and a long, brightly-colored skirt with sandals. Her eyes gave me the impression that she was very intelligent, curious, and intuitive. She carried herself with an air of aloofness; maybe that came with being the owner's wife. In another culture, she would have been smart, driven, and educated. But here she managed her children who cooked in the kitchen while she sold goods like textiles, soap, batteries, etc. She let out a good, rich laugh as she played with the children, but she was always aware of her place when her husband was around.

He returned to the teahouse just as my dinner arrived and sat at a corner table adjacent to mine. He was an arrogant man and very antagonistic toward me. I found my dahl baht less than tasty, and he took it upon himself to give me a hard time when it appeared that I didn't like it. I quickly drank an Indian beer called Tiger Beer, ate the chapati and some of the dahl to shut him up. Then I left. I didn't need the grief of a confrontation, and I was too tired to care what he thought of me.

I crawled into my sleeping bag around 7:45 p.m., read my book, wrote in my journal, and waited for the building to quiet down enough so I could sleep. Writing in my journal kept me grounded in my reason for being here. I could record the day's events and sort out the issues that were plaguing me back home. I, also was working on the future with new goals that would inevitably change my life.

The sounds of children playing, people talking in the restaurant below, and the bus driver and his mechanic doing repairs continued for a couple of hours. I could smell the bus's diesel exhaust, the kitchen fire, the pigeons, and the musty, dry odor of the room all mixed together. A pigeon coop was outside my window that I hadn't seen in the dark of my arrival. All night, the birds fought, cooed, and chased other birds on the teahouse roof. Since the roof was made of tin, their claws were like fingernails on a blackboard! This odd combination of noises went on most of the night. I had to laugh at the situation. What else could I do? I put in my earplugs and went to sleep.

Around 4:00 a.m., one of the bus drivers started his rig. I couldn't figure out why, since the bus didn't have to leave until 6:00 a.m. He shut it off after about fifteen minutes, blew the air horn five or six times, and walked away with his buddy, laughing. I think they were drunk. Everything was quiet until 5:15 a.m. when he started it again. The dogs started barking, the pigeons cooed, and people rose and began talking—so I got up and read my book. The sun was beginning to come up and with it, the first day of my trek what a day it would be.

I decided to mediate and prepare for the day and taking some time to reflect on the previous five days' events, I realized that something was very different in this area of Nepal. I felt I was seeing a different side of the Nepali people. Maybe it's the people of the Kanchenjunga region who are different, or maybe I was seeing them differently. They weren't at all like Tashi, my Sherpa guide on the first trip. Here, they were lazy, cynical, and a little angrier at life in general. There wasn't as much tourism here either, and I may have appeared as an intrusion too. Whatever it was, I felt an air of unfriendliness in this area.

As I thought about Tashi, I smiled. He had grown up in the region near Mt. Everest where his kinfolk are famous for their climbing and guiding skills. Sherpa is the name of Tashi's tribe, which originally lived near Tibet. The tribe migrated to the higher, eastern peaks and valleys of the Himalayas after being driven out by stronger tribe's centuries ago. Because they live in the highest regions of Nepal, Bhutan, and Tibet they can reach high summits without oxygen and make excellent guides. Tashi's name was "Tashi Lama Sherpa." Most Sherpas only use one name, but the government didn't like that, so the guides have adopted Sherpa as their last name.

Morning meditation often sets the tone for the day. I can let my mind become light and positive and see the possibilities. Focusing on purpose and gratitude alone will put me on the right track and into an adventurous mood. Today was going to be one adventurous day for sure.

GETTING LOST

As I awoke from my meditation, I didn't have a clue just how interesting—how much more than I had bargained for—the next few days would be. Oh well—I had wanted my Indiana Jones adventure; up to now, it had been tame, but an adventure nonetheless. The maps I had purchased in Kathmandu showed trails leading out of Cavalli to Taplejung, but I didn't know where the trailhead was.

I gathered my toothbrush, toothpaste, a bar of soap, and a towel and looked for a place to clean up. While brushing my teeth at the local waterspout across the street from the teahouse, I stood next to the young soldier who had helped me the night before. When I asked for directions to the trailhead, he took me about fifty yards away to the edge of a riverbed that, in the spring, must have swollen enormously with winter snowmelt. It was a good hundred yards across and fifteen to twenty feet deep at the bank. The present water flow was only twenty yards wide and the prettiest color of turquoise I had ever seen, indicating that its mineral content must be very high. Even though it was running at a low depth, the current appeared to be very fast. The young soldier pointed to a plank footbridge that crossed the river just upstream from our position and then to a tall mountain directly above the bridge and said that Taplejung was that way.

An hour later, before leaving, I had a Clif bar for breakfast and mixed some iodine tablets in my water bottles. While I was still at home, I had tested the weight of my pack (sixty pounds); somehow, today it felt much heavier. The mountain ahead of me looked much steeper than I wanted it to. I crossed the footbridge, being careful to avoid the missing planks.

I had only walked about half a mile by the time I reached the base of the mountain, and already, I was hot and sweaty. I stopped and removed my sack pants and long-sleeved shirt. I was about to resume walking when I noticed a young boy, who looked about seven years old, watching me from a few paces away. I didn't know how long he had been standing there, but he seemed very interested in my gear. I smiled and said, "Namaste," to which he responded in the same manner. When I asked him if this were the trail to Taplejung, he nodded yes and pointed up the trail into the thick foliage. He started walking the trail, and I followed. He seemed content to walk with me, though he never once uttered a word. Whenever I would stop to catch my breath, he would stop also. I noticed that he was carrying some books, so I gestured to him to let me see them, and he handed them to me. Both were very tattered and had been repaired with tape on their bindings. As I looked through them, I found that they were school books giving instructions in both English and Nepali. As I handed them back to him, he smiled, seeming to be very proud of them.

We had been walking for an hour or so when my watch beeped. It's a habit from the chaotic business world I work in to program it to do so on the hour. The boy stopped and quickly turned around to look at me, seemingly startled by the strange noise in the dense forest. When I realized what had caused the reaction, I showed him the watch and made a few adjustments in its programming so it would sound again. He found this delightful. Laughing, smiling, and pointing all the while, he was thoroughly enjoying the experience and so was I.

I was finally getting what I had come for—the smell of the forest and the sounds of the birds, squirrels, and other wildlife that you could hear but rarely see. And the children. Especially the children. The wide-eyed, filled with wonder and fun, children. I love the fact that in most cultures, they have no fear. They look and see what's there and become curious about the "what's and whys" while always smiling, with eyes darting from one object of interest to the next. I saw all these things and the absolute beauty of the Himalayas—the way they have been for millennia. In the cities, man is encroaching in a big way, but out here in the untouched regions, the people's lifestyles are pretty much the same as they have been for a very long time. The air is clean, and there is a wonderful peace in all you see. You can't come here and not feel touched by the serenity and spirituality.

Many of my family members and friends felt I was foolish for making this trip alone. At times, I felt I was also, but the complete sense of *knowing*, which eventually filled my heart, told me to go, to explore the world and myself, and I would be fine. Frequently in life, you can't find yourself without searching in places that are filled with some risk.

Risk is the basic commodity of life. When you risk with the intent of seeking growth and wisdom, God and the Universe will provide the tests and the choices. It's up to you to make decisions, learn and be tenacious.

Although the choices aren't always obvious or easy; at least we have the chance to choose. Not choosing is as much a choice as choosing. I've found that if I add a sense of adventure and imagination to my choices and decisions, then I approach them differently. With all choices come consequences, whether you like it or not. Having a good sense of acceptance of consequences goes a long way toward detachment from the outcome. If you are attached to a required result, you will almost always be disappointed. The last ingredient of this decision-making recipe is humor.

You need to acquire the ability to laugh at yourself because it helps lighten the load when times are hard.

As my little friend and I rounded a curve in the forest, a family home appeared before us. A few feet off the path was a small thatched roof hut, with cream-colored stucco walls and a tiny covered porch. Standing by the front door were the man of the house, a woman, who looked like his daughter, and her two children. When the man said something to the woman, she went inside and brought out a hand-woven, grass carpet square, laid it down, and pointed for me to sit on it. I did, and it felt good to take the weight off my feet. The family talked about my gear and pointed to my camera, so I took a picture of all of them. I'm sure I looked very foreign and strange to them.

After a few moments, I thanked them for the rest and started out again. Only a few hundred feet down the path, we came to a "Y" in the trail. The little boy went one way, stopped, and then pointed the other way for me. I hated leaving him, even though he had been my companion for only a short while. I liked having him along. We waved to each other and smiled; he turned and ran up the path, undoubtedly to tell his friends of his morning encounter. I started up my path, not knowing what small adventure was in store for me next. Suddenly, I felt rather naked, not knowing which way to go the next time there was a "Y" in the path. I decided to ask anyone along the way whether I was on the right trail. I also decided to keep taking the path that appeared to climb, rather than go down or laterally.

I ran out of water at about the time an old man stepped from another hut that sat next to the path. I held up my water bottle, turned it upside down, and asked for some water. After several sign language attempts, he understood and directed his wife, who had also appeared in the doorway, to fetch me some water. I added my iodine tablets, checked my watch, and made a mental note to let thirty minutes' pass before I drank any of it. I thanked them and left.

> RISK IS THE BASIC COMMODITY OF LIFE. WHEN YOU RISK WITH THE INTENT OF SEEKING GROWTH AND WISDOM, GOD AND THE UNIVERSE WILL PROVIDE THE TESTS AND THE CHOICES. IT'S UP TO YOU TO MAKE DECISIONS, LEARN AND BE TENACIOUS.

As the morning wore on, I mostly saw children, and they were fascinated with me. It was the time of day when they were all headed to a small country school somewhere. I walked along, enjoying the clean smell of the forest, attempting to avoid the huge spider webs that often spread across the trail. The spiders are large and poisonous and to be avoided at all costs. Luckily, the morning dew hung on the webs, making the spiders easy to spot.

I began to catch up to a small boy who was hiding behind each big tree that kept him a safe distance from me. The path wasn't more than a couple of feet wide, and amid the solid green foliage. I had purple hiking socks, tan shorts, a white T-shirt that had cartoon ducks on it, a red handkerchief rolled-up into a headband, and a large, green backpack. Plainly, my appearance was quite unusual and wonderfully intriguing to a five-year-old. Once we made eye contact and I smiled at him, he laughed mischievously and took off running. Moments later, when I rounded a small curve, six or seven children were waiting for me. When I saw them, I reacted with mock surprise and made them all laugh. I stopped and took a drink from my water bottle, slightly huffing from the steady climb.

The kids talked very fast to each other and giggled a lot while pointing to my socks and headband. As I looked around where we were standing, I realized that we were in someone's front yard. I walked a few paces to the front porch and sat down. When I took out my camera, they all got excited, obviously knowing what a camera was. They all laughed and shuffled about to get in the front of the picture. The boys were the most aggressive at this while the girls held themselves to the back and just giggled. The boys did all the talking. A middle-aged woman came down the trail with a large load of straw on her head and told the kids to move on to school, at least that's what I surmised she said. Suddenly, they waved goodbye and took off laughing and running. I asked the woman whether this was the trail to Taplejung. She nodded yes, so on up the trail I went.

I was traveling through a spectacular valley, and the morning was just as beautiful. Around me in near jungle-like conditions were splendid flowers of white, purple, pink, and yellow. Frequently, I crossed small streams that trickled through the bamboo forests. I tried to keep a steady pace, since I surmised it would take five to seven hours to get to Taplejung, and I didn't want to get there after dark.

I noticed that my feet were too warm. Since I had planned to be in a much colder climate, I wore heavy, all leather, Vasque hiking boots. The jungle atmosphere, however, was going to give me blisters, and I knew I was well on my way to having the first ones appear.

I thought about stopping for a time to apply moleskin, but I didn't. I would come to regret it later.

As a point of reference, I kept a ridgeline to my right and continued to climb. By noon, I had reached the upper basin of the valley, and I suddenly walked out of the jungle and right into the middle of a huge number of terraced rice paddies. The owner had cleared the land over many years, and almost all the natural vegetation was gone, except for the occasional tree here and there. The problem that became apparent instantly was that the trail disappeared. The paths on the front edge of the terraces were well-worn by the workers, but no single visible route lay upward.

A small army of workers was harvesting the rice, and numerous water buffalo were grazing on the grass between the rice paddies. The workers were about one hundred yards away from me, and as soon as I stepped out into the open and headed toward them, word spread quickly that someone new was in the neighborhood.

My pack was beginning to feel quite heavy, my feet hurt, and I was getting tired. I knew I needed to stop, eat, and rest. As I soon found out, climbing the forty to fifty individual rice paddies up the side of the mountain was neither easy nor fun. I tried to spot the man in charge, which wasn't hard since he did most of the yelling. Once I discovered who he was, I proceeded in his direction.

He may have been loud and gruff to his employees, but he was kind and helpful to me. He pointed to his farmhouse and said, "The trail to Taplejung there." I thanked him and started the hike up to the farmhouse. When I got there, three men were busy building a new home. The old one had collapsed into a heap of old adobe bricks and straw.

One of the workmen came over to see me when I sat down in the shade of a tree. He was the owner's son, between sixteen and eighteen years old. He was very curious about my gear, especially the Clif bar I started to eat. When I gave him a bite of it, he loved it, but to be gracious, he walked to a tree a few feet away, picked several mandarin oranges, and brought them to me. We attempted a conversation, and I took his picture. After about thirty minutes, I had to move on. He smiled, bowed, and pointed to where I could reconnect with the trail.

As you might expect, where there are rice paddies, there is a lot of water, and this hillside was no exception. There were many small, manmade ditches used for irrigation. It was hard work climbing up the four feet to each paddy, then walking thirty feet to the back of it, climbing up the four feet again, and doing this repeatedly. I stooped down to wet my headband in one of the streams when I heard, "What country are you?"

I looked to my left and saw three workmen stacking the rice stalks about twenty yards away. The older and more muscular young man stood out at once. Sweating from the hard work, his shirt was open, and he was wearing a red bandana tied around his head. His breathing was labored and his English broken, but we still managed to communicate. "I am from America. What country are you?" I asked teasingly. He laughed and shared my little joke with his friends. They laughed also.

"Where you go?" he continued.

"I am going to Taplejung. Am I on the right trail?"

"Yes," he said.

He turned, looked up the mountain, and pointed to the nearly vertical slope I was approaching. "Taplejung that way," he said.

"Thank you. Namaste," I replied.

"Namaste."

By now, the mid-afternoon sun was hot, and I was going through water rapidly. I had reached the end of the valley, and the view back down the mountain was beautiful—very green and lush. Some haze hung in the air, but you could see the valleys in the distance and the rolling foothills of the Himalayas. As I looked up ahead, the steep climb was daunting. The trail wound crookedly back and forth, then it disappeared into the trees. I started out and waved to the workers. They waved back and spoke to each other and laughed. I'm sure I was something of an oddity to them, but it added a little spice to their day, and they were enjoying it.

As I crisscrossed the mountain, the path would often come to a "Y," so I would have to make a choice, but on this mountainside, I had help.

Every time I would choose the wrong path, I would hear a whistle from far below. Turning to look down, I saw the man I had spoken with waving and pointing in the other direction, so I would turn around and go the other way. This happened three or four times during my ascent. When I reached a point where I knew I would lose sight of the workman, I turned and whistled to him and waved. He and his coworkers seemed happy and delighted that they had helped, and all four of them waved back and faintly shouted "Namaste!" I did the same, turned, and continued up the path and out of sight.

Help was coming from sources I didn't expect and when I didn't expect it. But it always came when I needed it most. I wasn't sure if there was a sense of security in that, but I did feel that I was being cared for by someone.

My feet were in bad shape after the hard climb up the ridge. The temperature was in the upper seventies, and I was sweating heavily. There wasn't a cloud in the deep blue sky, and the only sounds were my breathing and the pounding of my heart. By now, I had worn blisters on my blisters, so walking was becoming increasingly painful. I didn't want to look at the damage, but I knew I would have to sooner or later. I was hoping to top this ridge and see Taplejung on the other side, find a hotel for the evening, clean up, take care of my blisters, and get a hot meal. But the top of the ridge turned out to be a false summit, so I was very disappointed. Fatigue was setting in, and I needed some food, so I stopped in a small village. There were only four or five thatched roof huts with mostly women and children working and playing around them. I took off my pack, got out a Clif bar, drank some water, and rested in the shade of someone's front porch.

Word must have spread fast that someone new was there because soon I was surrounded by a small group of children and their mothers. In a typical, playful manner, all the children wanted to touch my gear or me.

When I finished eating, a little boy, who had been watching me, brought me a handful of mandarin oranges. This was the second time that day I had been given oranges, and I found them delightful. I ate several and put the rest in my pack for later. When I asked for directions from a young man, he pointed to a path that went horizontally around the mountain. I was grateful that I wasn't going up at a steep angle again since my feet needed a break.

By four o'clock, I reached the top of the next ridge, but no Taplejung was in sight. Before me lay another lush, green, tropical valley. It was becoming evident that I was lost. Although locals pointed in the direction I was going to get to Taplejung, I should have been there by now. I'd either taken a wrong turn along the way, or they didn't know what I was asking.

I had to laugh to myself; it would do me no good to be frustrated. *It's just another day in paradise*, I told myself. I knew I had about one and one-half hours of daylight left, so I was faced with the decision of where to spend the night. Not having prepared for this eventuality, I didn't have a tent or cooking gear. The next best thing was to find a farm where I could stay the night. As I surveyed the valley ahead of me, I could see a small hut with a big black water buffalo in a fenced enclosure. Since I didn't have many choices, the hut seemed like a good place to start.

As I approached the hut, a dog came up barking to warn me away. On my first trip, I had found that most dogs in Nepal are very scraggly and mean; this one was no exception. The more I tried to make friends, the more he snarled and bared his teeth. I had a piece of Clif bar in my pocket, so I tossed it to him. He sniffed it, licked it, and looked warily at me. Finally, he took the whole bite into his mouth and began to wag his tail. Kneeling, I stuck out my hand. Slowly, he came closer and sniffed me. Being reluctant to push it too far, I just let him get used to me for a while. When I reached out with my other hand and petted his head, he licked my hand, and we were fast friends.

Animals and I have always had a connection. I firmly believe they have an inherent instinct for who is a threat and who isn't. Luckily for me, my aura tells them I'm to be accepted. Wherever I go, the dogs, cats, and other varmints are attracted to me, and I love it.

Walking slowly toward the hut, I could now see that three people had been watching me interact with the dog. A man, his wife, and a little boy of five or six were standing in the doorway.

"Namaste," I greeted, and they said the same.

"Do you speak English?" I asked, and much to my astonishment, in a shy voice, the little boy said, "Yes, I do. A little."

"I am traveling to Taplejung, and it's taking longer than I had planned. I need a place to sleep tonight; may I stay here?"

He spoke in Nepalese to his parents and told them what I had said. They looked me over, spoke among themselves a little more, and then said something to the boy again.

"My father says you are welcome to stay, and we would be honored if you would eat with us."

I was awed by their hospitality and very grateful for the invitation. When I told the boy I would be very pleased to stay with them for the meal, they all smiled and talked to each other rapidly and excitedly. The mother gave the boy some instructions, and the father set about cleaning off the porch.

While they were making their preparations, I sat on the porch, took off my pack, and loosened my boots. It felt good just to sit and relax. I knew they would take good care of me; I felt safe and secure. I silently said a small prayer of gratitude to God for my good fortune and another safe day.

Being grateful and expressing it to God feels so good when you do it. I got this habit from my mother, and it's one I exercise regularly. I know how good it makes me feel when someone appreciates me and something I've done, so I can imagine God likes it just as much.

The boy sat next to me and told me his name was Chandra and that he was five years old. He was learning both English and Nepalese in his mountain school. Each day, Monday through Thursday, from ten to two o'clock, Chandra would attend classes. It took him thirty minutes to walk two valleys over to the little mountain schoolhouse. Chandra was very pleased with his English, and I could tell his father was very proud of him for speaking with me.

Chandra took me to where I would sleep for the night. About twenty yards from their house was a thatched roof enclosure for their 1200-pound black water buffalo. The bull looked as warily at me as I did at him. Chandra said I could sleep next to the bull, who he said was quite tame and warm. As I lay my pack down on the straw-covered floor and checked out my accommodations, I could only hope that the smelly bull didn't roll over in the night. I unpacked my sleeping bag and then cleaned up from the day of hiking.

A little later, I sat down next to a tall tree where I could look out over the valley below. Several small farms could be seen on adjacent hillsides with small strands of smoke rising from them also where dinners were being prepared. In the distance, I could hear roosters crowing and the occasional dog barking, but for the most part, it was quiet and extremely peaceful. I leaned back against the tree and closed my eyes. I let the silence overtake me, falling into a nice, meditative state. I felt my whole body relax and the pain in my feet subsided. I reveled in my body's ability to be resilient and recover. The air was cool, yet warm at the same time, almost perfect. The sense of *knowing* that I was safe and being taken care of was palpable and comforting.

At this moment, I had the perception of being the type of man I had always wanted to be. Everyone views his or her ideal self as confident, maybe somewhat adventurous and strong in body and spirit. In our normal lives, we don't always have the opportunity to feel this way, but when it all comes together, it's very rewarding. I was experiencing life the way I wanted and loving every minute of it. There haven't been too many times in my life when I could make that statement. While it prevailed, I meant to take advantage of every second.

I must have fallen asleep for a few moments, since the next thing I knew, Chandra was lightly touching my shoulder. "We are ready to eat," he said softly, with a smile on his face. His dark brown eyes sparkled, and his smile was warm and genuine. *What a delightful little human being*, I thought to myself as I rose to follow him into their home.

Seated on the hard dirt floor, we ate dahl baht and boiled cauliflower with our fingers. Chandra told me they were living on land that his grandfather had originally owned. They grew millet, rice, and beans. The old water buffalo did all the heavy work, and his father was very good at handling him. His mother wove baskets to sell at the market in Cavalli. Once a month, they all journeyed to Cavalli to sell their goods and buy the things they could afford. The steep trail I had just spent a whole day traveling was their highway to and from town. I couldn't imagine carrying their heavy loads both ways on that trail once a month in all kinds of weather. The father didn't wear any shoes, Chandra wore rubber sandals, and his mother wore a pair of old tennis shoes without any laces.

By the time we finished eating, it was dark, and we were sitting around a small fire in the corner of the hut. The nights get cold, so I was wearing my fleece pullover and a jacket. They wore light clothing and small light jackets. The woman only had on a sweater over her blouse. She kept working as the father and son talked to me. Sadly, women still have an incredibly hard life in Nepal. While we were talking, she washed the dishes in a large metal pan, brought in more firewood, carried in several buckets of water from the stream behind the hut, and fed the bull. During all that time, she never said a word. In fact, except for the words spoken when I first arrived, she didn't say anything until she bid me farewell the next morning.

By 8:00 p.m. I was very tired, but I still needed to tend to my feet. When I told Chandra, I was going to bed, he said they would be doing the same soon. I sat on my sleeping bag out on the grass-woven rug they had provided for me and pulled out my flashlight and first aid kit from my pack. Sitting in the cool mountain air, with the sounds of a few night birds and hundreds of bats in the tall rhododendron trees high above me, I proceeded to take off my boots and socks to survey the damage.

> I LET THE SILENCE OVERTAKE ME, FALLING INTO A NICE, MEDITATIVE STATE.
> I FELT MY WHOLE BODY RELAX AND THE PAIN IN MY FEET SUBSIDED.
> I REVELED IN MY BODY'S ABILITY TO BE RESILIENT AND RECOVER.

I didn't realize that the whole family was watching me over my shoulder in the dark. As I removed my socks, revealing badly blistered and bloody feet, they all gasped and spoke in hushed tones to each other. From the first aid kit, I took out antiseptic gauze wipes, cleaned the open sores, and then applied an antibiotic cream. Then I applied moleskin with holes cut to leave space over the blister so it could breathe and yet protect the skin. I washed my face with a baby wipe, and it felt so good. I knew I had gotten a little sunburned by how cool it felt.

The three of them left as I climbed into my sleeping bag. I read my book by flashlight for about fifteen minutes until I couldn't keep my eyes open any longer.

It had been a very long day, and sleep was only a couple of minutes away. The day had not ended like I had envisioned, but I had wanted an adventure and was getting it. Just as I was losing consciousness, I thought how lucky I was to be living life as I was and how grateful I was for the chance to do so. What new adventures would tomorrow bring? I loved the uncertainty.

WHERE THE HECK
AM I ANYWAY?

One of my favorite times of the day is the early morning hours just before sunrise. This particular morning will always rank among the most memorable. I awoke to the sound of bats way up in the trees. They could be seen against the still darkened sky, flitting from tree to tree and chirping up a storm. As the sky changed from black ink to deep blue and the stars began to disappear, the farm's roosters woke up and started doing their noisy early morning ritual.

Still lying in my sleeping bag, warm and comfortable, I could look down the valley to the east. Off in the distance through the cool early morning haze, the foothills of the Himalayas lay in different shades of gray and blue. The mist hung heavily in the valleys as another day in the mysterious land of Nepal slowly began. Soon I heard shuffling inside the hut and smelled a fire being brought back to life. Chandra was laughing in short giggles as morning teasing occurred between mother and son. "Just like in so many other households around the world," I thought. The sun made its presence known as rays of red and gold pierced the haze and caressed the treetops. The sky was turning a beautiful shade of blue, without a cloud in sight.

> MEDITATION CAN BRING POWERFUL TOOLS TO BEAR ON YOUR MIND. WE AREN'T CLOSE TO UNDERSTANDING HOW IT WORKS OR WHAT IT IS FULLY CAPABLE OF. WHEN YOU SLOW THE PACE OF THE MIND SO YOU CAN FOCUS FULLY ON THE MOMENT AT HAND YOU RECEIVE THE GIFT OF CLARITY.

The jungle's smells mixed with those of the farm, creating a delightful sensation. I've always liked the smell of a barnyard. The huge, black water buffalo lying next to me was watching the sunrise and chewing on its cud. He had an earthy fragrance of his own that was somehow comforting. Thankfully, he hadn't moved all night, but I had slept with one ear tuned to his movements. The gray whiskers on his nose gave me the feeling that he was old, seasoned, and probably very tame, but never having slept with a bull before, I had been uneasy nonetheless. The dirt in the area between the barn and the house was wet with dew. Small flies and other airborne insects began buzzing, and soon the air was filled with them. They greeted the sun and its rays of warmth, which came through the trees like golden arrows to the ground.

In a web built during the night, a spider sat motionless awaiting breakfast to arrive. His web stretched from the bull's horn to the post of the lean-to about eight inches above my head. These spiders were always a little disconcerting to me; their bodies were about the size of a silver dollar, and their front legs were two to three inches long. Not having a great liking for these critters anyway, I steered clear of them. However, as with spider webs everywhere, you could run into them because you couldn't see them. Chandra had arrived, and he giggled as he saw me looking at the spider. He picked up a stick, gathered in the spider, and took him off into the jungle. Ugh!

Nepalis take a small breakfast in the morning and a larger meal at 11:00 a.m. Then they wait until 7:00 p.m. to eat dinner. I could smell chapati being toasted and tea being brewed. As I slid out of my sleeping bag, my sore feet immediately reminded of their blistered condition, so I changed the bandages before I went any farther.

"Do you want chapati?" Chandra asked, peeking out the doorway.

"Yes, thank you," I replied with a smile.

One thing about the Nepalese, for the most part, they are a happy people, and I have found that this is the case most any time of the day. They sing and play with each other all the time. Some are grumpy like anywhere else in the world, but by and large, it's a jovial culture. I also discovered that the people in the countryside are far happier than their cousins in the city.

Chandra brought me a small basin of water, in which I washed my hands and face. As I entered the hut, the smoke was thick from the fire, and I had to bend over to be below the cloud that filled the area near the ceiling. Since the people cook inside their huts, the smoke rolls up and around the ceiling and out the nearest window. All the women of Nepal live and work in these conditions, and they develop nagging coughs early in life. The hut consisted of only two rooms with an adobe floor. The main room was for eating and other indoor household activities, and the other room was the bedroom for the entire family. Generally, large, thick, homemade, quilted mattresses and hand-woven blankets lay on the floor. Most of these homes have a picture of the Dalai Lama, but other than that, they are void of much decoration or furniture. What furniture there is will have been made by hand.

I sat on the floor, as I had the night before, and Chandra's mother brought me a metal plate with chapati, mandarin jam, butter, and a cup of chai.

It was fun to watch the family dynamics as they ate with me. The father was clearly the head of the household, and his wife took a distant second seat in authority. She didn't sit with us; forced by culture, she ate alone next to the fire. This situation is traditional, and it took me some time to get used to. The father, on the other hand, spoke through Chandra and asked many questions, such as: where I was from, where was I going, for how long, why was I alone, and what was America like. I got used to these questions, and for the most part, I liked answering them. In return, I asked some of my own. How old was he: thirty-four (he looked sixty-five); how long had he been married: nine years; had he ever gone to school: no, Chandra was the first in the history of the family to make that achievement.

He seemed pleased to answer my questions, and he genuinely seemed to like having me there, so this made for a very pleasant exchange. He teased me about my feet because he went everywhere barefoot, and his feet were like the best of leather-soled shoes. He also couldn't believe how much gear I was carrying, but when I told him how long I would be trekking at various altitudes, he understood.

I repacked my gear and prepared my water while they all watched. I almost hated to leave. Chandra and his parents had accepted me into their home, fed me, and treated me like family. I knew I would never see them again, and that was hard. When I gave Chandra a whistle I had brought, he beamed and blew it instantly after I showed him what it was. I wasn't so sure his parents would appreciate the gesture after a few hours, but for now, they accepted it warmly. When they weren't looking, I left 100 rupees on the table under the cooking utensils and plates.

We each held our hands together in praying fashion and said "Namaste," then I turned and walked down the path they said would eventually get me to Taplejung. I stopped and waved from a bend in the path a couple of hundred yards up the trail, and they were still standing, watching me and waved back.

The morning was warming up, and my feet were swollen and hurting, but I was still very glad to be here. A good feeling inside uplifted me—the kind that tells you that you are living the way God intended and that each day will only bring wondrous things your way. This feeling helped me be resilient. A good attitude; being happy and feeling tenacious help, too.

About an hour later, I stopped to sit and have some water. The trail was rough and littered with loose rocks, so it was hard on my feet. I tried to look ahead to see where the path went next. In the distance, high above a river, I could see a plank bridge crossing the valley. It was a great picture, so I unloaded my camera and took several black and white shots, and then, with another camera, a few color shots as well. I was carrying a tripod, around twenty rolls of black and white film, another fifteen rolls of color slide film, three cameras, three lenses, and assorted filters. Many of the photos I got made me glad that I had carried all the gear, even though there were times while climbing when I cursed the weight.

The trail's angle was constantly upward, although not very steep most of the time. Occasionally, though, I would round a bend and be faced with a long climb up to the top of the next ridge. This was the main highway of sorts and I would meet people every once in a while. The men would be carrying doko's—woven baskets placed on their backs and secured with straps around their foreheads and the tops of the baskets. They carry everything from grain, straw, beer, propane, blankets, etc., and it's not as easy as it looks. I tried it once and nearly fell over backward. Some of these men would smile toothless grins and say "Namaste," while others would look at me with wonder and curiosity. Around ten each day, I would encounter some children on their way to a school somewhere in the hills. They would always stop and giggle.

Unlike my first trip to Nepal in the Annapurna region, this trek didn't have the repetitiveness of terrain. On that trek, we would climb a ridge for about an hour, then drop down the other side, cross a roaring stream, meander through a beautiful bamboo forest, and then back up another ridge and repeat the process over and over. This time, it was a steady climb through some of the most beautiful jungle I'd ever been in. The lush greenery was so brilliant that it almost hurt my eyes.

Occasionally, I would break out of the jungle and have a wonderful view of the surrounding valleys and mountainsides. It was cool until noon, so I would keep a long-sleeved shirt on and then switch to just a T-shirt for the remainder of the afternoon.

Over the years, the Nepalese government has had work teams install black, industrial plastic pipe underground to carry water down from the snows above. The only problem is that the pipes crack with weather changes or when people and animals step on exposed sections. That allows dirt to get inside, so by the time the water is carried downhill through several cracks, it gets somewhat murky and unsanitary. You come across these pipes every so often sticking out of manmade concrete troughs. The pipe is only three inches in diameter, but it carries just the right amount of water to fill water bottles or basins for the locals. Because of the contamination, I hated drinking it, but I felt the iodine tablets would kill almost everything—at least I hoped they would. When I had planned this trip, I'd thought I'd be going into an area like Annapurna where bottled water and food were available at teahouses—Ah, the plans of mice and trekkers.

A couple of hours after filling my water bottles I came to the plank bridge I had seen earlier in the morning. It covered a span of about two hundred feet and hung from huge cables. The wooden planks were well-worn and broken or missing altogether in places. When I could see through the cracks and broken planks, my stomach did a butterfly dance. I have acrophobia, and must work at feeling calm in situations where there is a lot of open air, and it is a long way down. The only way to overcome this phobia is to be exposed to heights regularly so that you get used to them. Sweaty palms, butterflies, and a dry mouth are always just under the surface, though, ready to grab you more than you want. I had to jump over the missing areas and hold my breath, hoping that the plank I landed on would hold me. I clutched the heavy rope that ran along each side of the bridge and slowly made it across.

The river below was like many others I had seen in Nepal—the most beautiful turquoise color with white foam. When you added the green of the jungle, it made for a spectacular sight. These rivers drop very rapidly, so they were a whitewater rafter's dream. I was about 300 feet above the bottom of the gorge and didn't spend a lot of time looking down. Once on the other side, I treated myself to a Clif bar and a drink to celebrate making it across. Several of the locals walked by and over the bridge, carrying heavy loads while talking to each other and laughing. Their life is hard, but they still seem to enjoy it, despite dangerous crossings. On the other hand, I was probably the only one who found it scary.

I continued to ask people who passed whether I was on the right trail to Taplejung, and all nodded and pointed in the direction I was going. I looked at my map a couple of times; it didn't show this much distance between Cavalli and Taplejung, but then, who knows how accurate it was to begin with? I just settled into a steady pace that my feet could endure and kept going. I was on vacation after all, and I wasn't going to let a little detour, if it was a detour, keep me from enjoying myself.

Actually, I was having fun. It was a blast to be in a place where I didn't know anyone, relying on my tenacity, instincts, and the information available. It was a challenge I enjoyed. I was picking up more of the language as I went along too, and that helped a lot.

Around noon, I entered a small village. At first, I thought I had made it to Taplejung, but I soon discovered it was just a small cluster of huts that were situated together along the trail. There was a small teahouse with an outdoor table, and some of the local people were having lunch there. There were many children, and as soon they spotted me, they all came running up, happy to have a new diversion in their day.

I can remember when I was a kid that occasionally, a bum would stray from the railroad tracks where he had been riding the slow freights and wander through our small town. I always hung out with two other neighborhood kids, and we would run up to those fellows and ask them questions. They always seemed so different—different from the everyday people we were used to, at least. It excited us to meet someone who obviously had a different slant on life and how it should be lived. It was times like that when my *imagination* ran rampant. What was their life like? What kind of adventures were they having, living on the road? Imagination is a wonderful tool for child and adult alike, and we need to use it more to see a broader view of possibilities.

I'm sure that is how I appeared to these children—someone who was out in the world, experiencing it from a different angle than they were. Each time this kind of occasion occurred, and it occurs many times on treks like this, I felt welcome and cared for, if not a little embarrassed by how much attention I received. For the most part, the Nepali don't exhibit any fear of you; they seem to accept you right off and are just curious about you—the people in Cavalli being the odd exception.

One of the joys this day was discovering that the teahouse had packaged Ramen noodles like we have back home. I took off my pack and ordered some; the noodles would have to be boiled so they would be safe, even if the water were treated. The smell of the broth was heavenly, and they tasted better and better, especially since I had been living off Clif bars for a couple of days. To have a hot meal was very welcome at this point, and my feet needed the rest. I stayed for about an hour and then had to leave. The kids followed me down the path for a while and then stopped and waved and yelled "Namaste" to me. Barefoot and in tattered clothing, they were just as happy as kids who had all the conveniences of the modern world; maybe more so. In many ways, these children were better off by far.

As the day wore on, I noticed a black dog on the trail behind me. I was a little leery of it. On my first trip three years earlier, the dogs in Kathmandu would fight over garbage, and they were all scarred and mangled from many fights. You didn't dare pet them because they might bite you. This one looked ragged but in a different way. He looked lost and hungry, and his coat was full of small weeds and dried mud. I started keeping an eye out for him, not quite sure of his motives. At first, I thought he was just going home from a few days of chasing small squirrels and playing in the forest, but after he had followed me for more than a couple of hours, I figured he was just a wild dog.

At one of my increasingly frequent rest stops, he slowly came close to me and lay down. He was about ten feet away and

IT WAS TIMES LIKE THAT WHEN MY IMAGINATION RAN RAMPANT. WHAT WAS THEIR LIFE LIKE? WHAT KIND OF ADVENTURES WERE THEY HAVING, LIVING ON THE ROAD? IMAGINATION IS A WONDERFUL TOOL FOR CHILD AND ADULT ALIKE, AND WE NEED TO USE IT MORE TO SEE A BROADER VIEW OF POSSIBILITIES.

looking about as wary of me as I was of him. While I was eating, his nose went up in the air to see what he could smell of my food. Breaking off a piece of a cookie, I tossed it toward him. He got up slowly, meandered over to it, and smelled it. He looked up at me and at the clump of food, and then he ate it cautiously. I noticed a faint wiggle of his bushy tail and knew that he approved. He sat down, watching me closely as he licked his lips and smelled the air again.

This little ritual was repeated over the next two or three rest stops until he was sitting beside me panting, acting like a dog from any other part of the world that wants what you're eating. He seemed friendly, so I reached out and brushed the coarse black hair out of his eyes. He wasn't a Chow, but some of that ancestry was in him somewhere. Mostly, he was a mixture of many breeds. Before long, he had accepted me, and I was less afraid of him. It felt good to have a companion again. One of the nice things about having animals as friends is they don't complain or talk back. This pup was no exception. He seemed happy to have made a friend too, especially one who gave him food.

In the late afternoon, it was becoming apparent that I once again was going to need a place to spend another night, but I was beginning to smell so bad that I didn't want to approach anyone in my current odorous condition. I had been sweating heavily in the afternoon heat, and I needed a bath. When I came upon a small stream, I followed it until I was forty or fifty yards away from the path. I removed my pack and proceeded to take my clothes off. When I sat down in the cool water, it felt so good. If you've never taken a bath in the wilderness, you're missing one of the great joys of life.

I was reminded of a time when I was fishing with my dad on the Gunnison River in Colorado. Around ten in the morning, I was standing in the middle of the river in my waders when out of the corner of my eye I saw someone upstream. About seventy-five yards away, a man was moving quickly, but gingerly, into the water. Upon closer examination, I discovered, much to my amazement, that it was my father and he was totally naked! He was laughing and waving at me, obviously enjoying the shock value of the moment. I didn't want to stare, but it was not what I had expected of my "Old Man." He had bathed quickly because the water was cold and then ran back into the bushes to dry and dress. Now, sitting in the cool stream, the memory brought a smile to my face, and I thought how Dad might now laugh at me for doing the same thing.

As I bathed, I got used to the temperature of the water and began to enjoy the experience. Being completely naked in the wilderness is fun all by itself; add the little boy in me and rushing water and you have the ingredients for play. I started splashing water on the dog sitting on the bank. He didn't like it at first, but then with my laughter and playful attitude, he got into the swing of things. He ran back and forth on the bank, barking at me and wagging his tail. Eventually, he was soaking wet.

When I stopped playing, I slowly walked over to him and petted his head. I coaxed him into a small still pool near the edge and took out my bar of soap and proceeded to give him a bath too. At first, he was apprehensive, but then he began to enjoy the attention. As he got used to the process, I scrubbed him down, and he enjoyed the scratching that his skin received. As dogs will do, he moved his hind leg in a scratching motion when I would hit a particularly itchy spot. I had brought my scissors to trim my beard, so I took them out of my pack and cut a lot of his mangled hair from behind his ears and his legs. All of this must have taken the better part of an hour.

When he dried off, he looked pretty. It's funny that with most creatures, human or otherwise, when you've been cleaned up and received a little tender loving care, you act differently. You feel better about yourself. It was no exception for this pooch. He strutted down the trail ahead of me when we started again, whereas before he would lag behind me. He acted happy, and I loved it.

The evening was fast approaching, and I knew that having him along was going to make it difficult to find a porch or a barn to sleep in. I had walked for about thirty minutes when I happened upon a small Buddhist temple. As near as I could tell, there wasn't anyone there, so I quietly entered to look around. This was the first sign of any religious edifice I had seen in this part of the country.

The building was very old and rundown, but the grounds around it and the inside were very clean. The temple was made of deteriorating red brick with moss and vines growing up its sides. The wooden shingle roof was also in need of repair. It sat in a grove of very tall trees and appeared to be the only building. As I went up the three steps of the entry, I could smell jasmine incense burning, so I knew I wasn't alone. I approached the altar where a human-sized statue of Buddha sat in the traditional pose, smiling back at me.

It felt good to take my pack off and sit down on the woven grass mat in front of the statue. In the late afternoon air, birds were flying through the open windows in the upper area, while flies and other insects buzzed through the last warm rays of the sun. My dog lay down a few feet away and went to sleep. I crossed my legs, closed my eyes, and allowed myself to slip into that wonderful state of mind that had become so familiar in my meditations.

The calm and serene feeling that most of us experience when we are close to our individual deities had become my natural state of mind over the last week. As I sat in this wonderful old temple, my mind became quiet, and my body relaxed. I was aware of my breathing, my heart pumping, and the sensation of warm air against my skin. As I took long, slow, deep breaths to relax, I noticed a new lightness to my being. *This is something new*, I thought, and it was very enjoyable. With my eyes closed, I slowly became aware that I was floating and that the scene around me, visualized in my mind, was moving down and away from me. It was then I recognized that I was having an out-of-body experience.I could see myself seated in front of the statue and the dog asleep on my left side. I was acutely aware of the air, temperature, sounds, and smells, and how very calm I was, almost euphoric. It seemed as though as soon as it started, it stopped, and I was opening my eyes, looking around the temple where now there were a few candles burning. More time had elapsed than I had thought since it was almost dark. I was rested, comfortable, and felt very safe. Places of religion, spirituality, or metaphysics evoke a calmness that is eerie and yet comforting. Oddly, I felt as if I had been here before.

As I stood and stretched, I became aware that I was not alone. Off to my right, standing in a dark shadow, was a small Buddhist monk.

When he saw that I had discovered him, he stepped into the candlelight. The palms of his hands placed together in the traditional prayer fashion, he bowed slightly and said, "Namaste." I returned the greeting and smiled.

"You have a wonderful meditation in my temple?"

"Yes, I have. It was a little more than I was prepared for. Say, you speak excellent English."

"Thank you. I have studied at the University in Kathmandu," he said with a smile and much pride.

"I appreciate the use of your temple, although I have stayed longer than I had originally planned," I said.

"It has grown dark since your arrival; would you like to spend the night here before moving on?" he asked knowingly.

"Yes, I would. I was wondering where I was going to sleep tonight. I appreciate your offering."

"Please come to my room in the back. I will prepare dinner for both of us, and you can tell me where you are from and where you are going." He gestured for me to follow him through a deep crimson curtain into an area behind the statue.

I wondered how long he had been standing watching me meditate since he knew when I had arrived. The whole setting had a curious feeling about it, but it also felt safe. *A strange combination of feelings*, I thought.

As we entered the back room, I was greeted with a wonderful array of sensations. The monk had a pot of vegetable stew on the small grating over the fire in the corner, and the room was well-lit by a half-dozen candles that each cast its own set of dancing shadows. It was only one room, but it contained everything he would need. Off to the left was a small alcove that had a mattress with bedding on the floor. The fireplace in the center of the far wall had a table to its right with cooking utensils, pots and pans, and some additional vegetables cut up, ready for the pot. To the right of the table was a small window that looked out into the courtyard behind the temple. In the room's center were several large pillows on a woven mat. The short wooden table between the pillows held two tin plates and two cups for tea and another candle. It appeared that I was expected. On the walls were brass plates with Buddha's face imprinted on them, and several small hand-woven pictures of Buddha were framed and hung on each side of the plates. The walls were cream-colored, and the curtain that he used to block off the sleeping area, as well as the one at the window, was like the one at the entry to the room, a deep, dark red that was almost crimson. Everything was clean and neat and in its place. The monk obviously was as fastidious in his home as he was in his religion.

My dog had entered the room behind me; he lay down in the corner and proceeded to watch us while trying to keep his eyes open. The monk motioned for me to sit on one of the pillows. I took off my boots, placed them by the dog, and sat down.

"You seem to have a companion," he said, looking at the dog.

"Yes, I made friends with him earlier today. I gave him a bath when I took my own, and he seems to have adopted me."

"I thought he looked very clean. It was nice of you to care for him. Most Nepali don't hold too much regard for dogs. But where you come from they must."

"Yes, I am from America, and I have had several dogs as pets over my lifetime. They always offer unconditional love, and I try to give it back in the same way. I have always felt that animals are to be treasured."

"Some, like the cow, are revered here, as you probably know. But food is scarce, and often an animal is just another mouth to feed. I would like to see America someday; it sounds like a fascinating country. Although I don't know if I could ever leave my beloved temple," he said, opening his arms wide and looking around him with a big smile.

This was the first chance that I had to study him. He was average height for a Nepali, about 5' 1" and a little on the plump side. His head was shaved, and he wore the traditional crimson robe, a white T-shirt, and sandals. When he spoke, he stood very still with his fingers woven together and held in front of his stomach. He had a quiet, soft, round face, deeply tanned, and a big smile filled with very white teeth, which was unusual.

He walked over to the table, gathered the last of the vegetables, and tossed them gently into the stew pot. He proceeded to stir the mixture with a wooden spoon. As he stood and stirred, he looked at me curiously and asked, "You wouldn't happen to have any pepper with you?"

"Why, yes, I would," I said, somewhat surprised, yet pleased that I could offer something to the meal. I rose and went to the temple to retrieve my pack. I put it in the corner of the room and opened a pouch that contained items to placate my Western sense of comfort, spices among them. I handed him a small plastic container that had pepper in one end and salt in the other.

While he finished preparing our meal, he told me his name was Pasang, and he was originally from a small town near Lumbini where Buddha was born. There, in the southern part of Nepal, where my trip would take me during the last ten days of my trek, it is much warmer. He shared that although he liked the mountains, they were just a little too cool for his warm blood. One thing was certain; he sure liked his salt and pepper like they did in southern Nepal.

We didn't say anything to each other for a few minutes. Pasang busied himself preparing our dinner, and I watched. His movements were slow, deliberate, confident, and memorized from years of repetition. As night arrived and a familiar coolness filled the air, I realized that I was chilled, so I opened my bag to take out my sack pants and a fleece pullover.

Now it was his turn. As I retrieved my clothes and straightened up my camera equipment, he watched me. I didn't see him watching me, but I could feel it. As I looked up, he said, "You are very well-organized."

"Well, I have always been one of those people who tries to be prepared. However, I feel I have overdone it on this trip. My pack is heavier than I would have liked. Do I have a few minutes before we eat?"

"Yes, but why do you ask?"

"My feet have taken a beating over the past couple of days, so I need to tend to them." He nodded and moved closer.

I took out my first aid kit, sat on a small bench along one wall, and removed my socks. I used one of the baby wipes to wash my hands and another for each foot. With my scissors, I cut the blisters open and removed the dead skin so I could apply a bandage. As I was doing this, he brought me a cup of chai. Then he sat at the table to drink a cup of his own and watch me.

"Your feet are causing you great discomfort. Is there anything that I can do?" Pasang asked.

"No, I think I have everything here that I need but thank you for asking. Being able to stay here and eat with you is a welcome relief. I appreciate your hospitality, and I am so glad you speak English so we can talk."

"Why are you in Nepal?" he asked softly.

"I came here three years ago, and I liked your country and its people very much. I trekked in the Annapurna region with a friend of mine and wanted to see some more."

"I think it is much more than that," he said with a smile.

"Oh," I said. "What makes you say that?"

"The experience you had in my temple this afternoon."

He was so calm and matter-of-fact in his appraisal of me that I laughed aloud. It was either out of a sudden small pang of nervousness or one of those times when someone has the upper hand in a conversation, and you don't know what to say, but whatever it was, I felt very vulnerable.

He sensed this and said, "You are obviously a man in search of higher purpose, and your spirituality is on a quest for answers. I am most grateful that Buddha has brought you to me. You can relax, stay as long as you like, and we will explore these things."

As I sat and watched the light from the candles and the fire cast a small group of shadows on the walls, an extraordinary warmth came over me—a *knowing* that I had arrived at the right place at the right moment and was being guided with safety and precision. For the unaware, synchronicity is very often hard to recognize, but this one was so blatant that anyone could have seen it. I sat down on the pillows as Pasang served the stew and chapati and was filled with anticipation of what was yet to come.

For a few moments, we ate in silence, and then he laughed a belly laugh and slapped the table gently. "I would imagine that you were quite a sight on the path today. We don't get many visitors like you here. You will be the talk of the villages for weeks to come."

I proceeded to tell him of the family I had stayed with the night before and of their hospitality and charm, of the children in the village where I ate my mid-day meal, and about the people I had seen on the trail the past two days.

"Where did you acquire your friend?" he inquired.

"I got to know him earlier today. He had been following me, so I coaxed him to me by feeding him. When I took a bath in a stream this afternoon, I bathed him too, and he really liked it. I felt he needed a friend and a little love, and love, well, that's something I have a lot of."

"As we spoke of earlier, most dogs in Nepal are wild and do as they please," he said softly. "This one has taken a liking to you, which is unusual. He must sense that you are a good person. Animals have that ability, you know. You, too, have an ability to *know*."

This statement set me back for a second. Pasang had indeed seen into my soul and into my heart, but how? Noticing my amazement, he continued, "You are a man of insight and tenacity, but you don't credit yourself for it. As you meditated this afternoon, I too entered a meditative state. I saw that you are on a journey that is opening many doors of enlightenment to you. God is in touch with you and is guiding you. The people you are meeting are not by chance, for it is you who is inviting them to you by approaching your journey with a great love of adventure and of mankind."

He continued, "You are discovering the essence of life. To leave the known and to walk into the unknown without fear is called faith, and faith is what your journey is all about."

He had filled my soup bowl twice during our conversation, so I was now full. There was some left over, so I asked whether it would be okay with him to give it to my dog. He smiled and nodded. The food was greeted with a panting tongue and a wagging tail, and it disappeared in a few seconds.

I helped Pasang clean up from the meal, and then we both stepped into the temple, where he lit some candles. There were no glass windows or doors to close off the temple from the cold of night, so a chilly breeze softly blew through the tall, open, ancient structure.

We sat on the front steps where I could see the fabulous Nepalese sky filled with more stars than you can imagine. Around us, no light could be seen from any town, city, or farm. Only the faint glow of the candles behind us in the temple gave any light to our surroundings at all. The dog curled up next to me and put his head on my leg. It felt warm and soothing, and as I stroked his back slowly, he went to sleep, after a couple of small whimpers of approval.

We sat in silence for quite a while, looking at the stars. "I have had one other out-of-body experience like the one you witnessed this afternoon," I said without being asked.

"Yes, and what was it like?"

"I was driving in my car on a busy highway near my office. A friend and mentor of mine named Pete told me to read a book by an author who explored these experiences, and the idea intrigued me. I decided to try to have one on my own, but I didn't really expect anything to happen. Anyway, as I was driving, I took a deep breath and told myself to quiet my mind and to relax, which I did. What happened next was quite unbelievable. I slowly began to rise and move above my body, where I could see myself driving, from behind. For a moment, I was very calm, warm, and serene, but suddenly, I realized I was going 65 mph, and all I could see was my body below me, not the traffic surrounding or ahead of me. I arrived back in my body with a jolt. I put the windows down to get some fresh air and to catch my breath, which was suddenly hard to get. My heart was racing, and I burst out laughing at my experience.

———————

HE (PASANG) WAS QUIET FOR A FEW MINUTES AND THEN SAID, "ENCOUNTERS LIKE THESE ARE THERE FOR THE ASKING, IF THE INQUIRING MIND IS READY, AND THEY ONLY HELP TO CONFIRM THAT OUR SPIRIT OR SOUL IS VERY POWERFUL, ABUNDANT, AND ALWAYS PRESENT. FORTUNATELY, YOU HAVE OPENED YOURSELF TO THE LOVE OF THE UNIVERSE AND OF GOD. YOU ARE WILLING TO BE SHOWN THESE THINGS, AND SO THEY WILL COME TO YOU. IT IS THE

STRENGTH OF YOUR INTENTIONS THAT MAKES YOU DESERVING AND WORTHY. WE ALL HAVE THE SAME KNOWLEDGE THAT IS BROUGHT WITH US INSIDE OUR SOUL, BUT NOT ALL OF US OPEN OURSELVES TO REMEMBER. WITH THE DAY-TO-DAY ACTIVITIES FILLING OUR MINDS, WE OFTEN CAN'T HEAR THE SMALL HINTS GIVEN TO US TO SLOW DOWN, GET INTO OUR HEARTS, AND SEE WHO WE REALLY ARE AND WHY WE ARE HERE. THIS IS ONE OF THE LESSONS OF YOUR JOURNEY. YOU NOW HAVE THE SURROUNDINGS TO SLOW DOWN AND LISTEN. I LEFT KATHMANDU MANY YEARS AGO TO ACCOMPLISH THE SAME THING. NOW, I AM BLESSED WITH AN ASTONISHING RELATIONSHIP WITH GOD AND WITH MY SELF. I WISH YOU THE SAME."

WITH THAT, WE SAT QUIETLY, BOTH OF US REFLECTING ON WHAT HAD BEEN SAID. THE NIGHT SKY WAS FILLED WITH ITS USUAL MAGNIFICENT ARRAY OF STARS, AND SOME STARS OCCASIONALLY FELL, LEAVING A TRAIL FOR A FEW SECONDS. THE AIR WAS COOL, BUT THE DOG'S HEAD NESTLED ON MY LEG KEPT ME WARM. ACTUALLY, AS I THOUGHT ABOUT IT, I WAS WARM ALL OVER. NOT FROM MY CLOTHING OR THE DOG, BUT FROM THE INNER

WARMTH OF UNDERSTANDING. THE EXCITEMENT OF PASANG'S WORDS MADE MY HEART PUMP A LITTLE FASTER, AND MY WHOLE BODY SEEMED WARM AS A RESULT. I WAS OBVIOUSLY EXCITED TO HAVE THIS DISCUSSION WITH A MAN OF SUCH DEEP UNDERSTANDING.

"I have told this story to a couple of disbelieving friends, and I almost don't believe it myself. When I arrived at your temple today, I was so tired, and a good meditation sounded very soothing. I sat down, got quiet, and almost immediately, the second experience occurred. This time, though, it was wonderful. I was relaxed throughout and felt refreshed when it was overAlthough, I was a bit startled when you appeared."

"Would you like some tea?" he asked. "I am going to get some for myself."

"Yes, I would. Thank you. Can I help?"

"No, I will be back soon. Please, sit and enjoy the moment."

As I turned and watched him shuffle through the temple, his sandals gently scraping the old stone floor with each step, I had the feeling of being in a movie, and I heard soft music playing in my head. It was a Rod Stewart song that had held strong significance for me in the past called "Have I Told You Lately That I Love You." I loved and missed the woman whom the song reminded me of. *It would have been nice*, I thought, *to have shared these experiences with her.* But I knew this was an experience I needed for myself. I knew I would eventually have to face the unfinished business I had with her, but right now, I had other lessons to learn.

The feeling of being in a movie and seeing myself from a short distance away was puzzling to me, and as Pasang returned with the chai, I asked him about it. "You have seen movies, haven't you?"

"Oh, yes. I went to one in Kathmandu. But they show the same movie over and over. It features one of our national heroes, and the Nepali never tire of it."

"I've seen it also, on my first trip to Nepal. I enjoyed it, but the seats were too close together for my bigger Western body," I said laughing.

"Why do you ask?" Pasang questioned.

"Well, I have a strange recurring sensation, and please don't laugh, but it's like I see myself in a movie from a short distance away. I hear music playing in the background too. It's the oddest feeling. Not quite like the out-of-body experience we spoke of earlier, but similar."

Pasang responded softly, "We have been taught that we all have an observing self and that it helps guide us by having the wonderful ability to see things in a larger picture. It helps to observe yourself in certain situations so you can make decisions based on seeing all the facts and not just the ones pressed up against your nose."

"Okay," I replied. "But what if it happens when you are not really faced with a difficult situation where you have to make a decision? In mine, I see myself cruising along driving, walking, or just sitting, reading a book."

"I feel you have been struggling with some major issues in your life and that's why you are on this journey. By letting you see yourself in the broader picture, you are being shown that the issues are a small part of your life. Yes, they are important things that you must take care of, but in the overall scheme of life, they are but a stepping stone. Your observing self is giving you the opportunity to realize that you can be happy if you let yourself."

"I had not thought of it that way, but it does make sense," I said softly. "Thank you."

"You're welcome. You look very tired, and it's getting late. Let me show you where you can sleep."

"Yeah, suddenly I do feel very drained. But it's a good feeling," I said, smiling.

We had talked for almost an hour before we both fell asleep. As I snuggled down in my sleeping bag next to the small fire in Pasang's living quarters, I felt very blessed to have happened upon such a wonderful man. To be here in the wilderness of Nepal and find an ancient temple tended by a single individual with whom I could communicate so well and from whom I would learn so much, obviously was not a coincidence. I fell asleep *knowing* that once again my trip was providing me with everything I had asked for and more.

THREE SCHOOL INSPECTORS...
REALLY?

I awakened to the soft chanting of prayers coming from the temple. It was a pleasant way to wake up. I eased out of my sleeping bag, pulled on my sack pants and a sweatshirt, and wandered sleepily into the temple.

Several Nepali were seated, some were kneeling, and still others were standing. Some had brought marigolds to place on the Buddha altar. Pasang had incense burning in a corner, and he was praying off to one side. I decided to join him, so I sat in the lotus position, closed my eyes, and took several deep breaths. I felt very calm and rested, so I achieved the alpha state of mind quickly. The smell of the fragrant incense, the chanting of mantras echoing in the temple, and the cool morning air all made for a very spiritual setting and awe-inspiring way to start the day.

Nepalese are mostly Hindus, Buddhists, and Muslims, with some Christians sprinkled in. All live in this tiny country without any religious wars. They don't all agree with each other's perspective, but they do respect one another's right to pray to whomever or whatever one wants. Often, you will see Hindu and Buddhist temples in the same square. These people have been raised to know that no matter what God you pray to, it all boils down to spirituality, love of God, love of Self, and Self-expression or creativity.

Meditating and praying have one side effect of which I am particularly grateful: clearing my mind of chaotic thought. Our bodies have a built-in mechanism that reduces the cycles per second of brain wave activity by just closing our eyes. Combining this with deep breathing techniques used by most who meditate and the result is a mind/body connection that allows us to clear our minds and be virtually free of chaotic thoughts. In this state, you can come closer to the spiritual state of mind that we are all searching for. You can hear that little mental voice that speaks to you only when you slow down enough to hear it. At this level of meditation, we all enter a different reality than we experience the rest of the day. You can learn how to achieve that reality in your waking hours to allow yourself to move in and out of the multiple realities of your day, making life much simpler and more pleasant. We all share other people's realities as we enter and exit different offices and businesses or while we are in traffic; remaining meditative and calm, outside the realms of anger and frustration, can eliminate those emotions.

About thirty minutes had passed when I felt it was time to open my eyes. When I did, I discovered that the temple was completely empty, except for me and man's best friend, who was curled up against my right thigh. His big brown eyes were looking up at me; I reached out and scratched his side. He rolled over on his back so I could continue scratching his belly. I was pleased to have him along during this part of my trek; life is a little more complete when you have an animal as a friend and companion.

I rose and walked to the front entrance. The valley that stretched below was bathed in the morning mist, and I could see spider webs with dew hanging heavy on their strands spanning the space between two trees. The dog and I stretched and yawned at the same time. It made me laugh to think how different and yet how similar we were.

I felt a hand gently squeeze my shoulder and turned to see Pasang holding a tray with two cups of steaming chai on it. He was smiling—no, he was beaming.

"Well, you certainly look happy this morning," I said.

"Yes, I slept well, prayed well, and all is right with the world this morning," he replied with a grin.

"I must have meditated very deeply this morning myself. When I joined you, there were some people in the temple, but when I opened my eyes, everyone was gone, and I hadn't heard any of them leave."

"When I got up to do some duties, you were very comfortable, so I decided to let you meditate and wait for you," he said as we sat down on the front steps of the temple. "Some of our people were very surprised to see you praying with them. We don't get many visitors like you here. They will be talking about you for some time."

I sat for a few moments and then said, "I don't want to leave this morning, but I have to get to Taplejung and then back to Badraphur in time for my flight to Kathmandu."

"I understand," he said. "It is often sad how we set ourselves up to rush through some experiences, but at least you have had the experience. It has been very nice having you stay with me. I have enjoyed our talks and will pray that you find whatever you want from life. Before you go, please let me prepare you something to eat. You can get your equipment ready while I do that."

"Thank you; that would be great. Would you have a little for the dog, too?"

"Yes," he laughed. "We will take care of him too."

It took about an hour to wash my face, repack my gear, and eat. As Pasang walked me to the edge of his compound, I felt a deep sense of sadness at leaving. He must have sensed this because he said, "We will meet again someday; maybe not in the same way, but I know this to be true. Do not look upon this time sadly." With that, he bowed, placed his hands together, and said, "Namaste."

I did the same, smiled at him, turned, and started down the path with my dog bouncing happily behind me. I didn't turn around to wave because I knew if I did, I would start to cry. My visit to his temple and the hospitality I had received would be a pleasant memory for all my life. His words of enlightenment would stay with me, and I would pass them on to many other people as my life progressed. Although he had been a very small part of the time I would spend on this planet, he had filled me with wondrous thoughts—thoughts I would consider for a long time to come. The hours of conversation with him came out of nowhere. I like it when life does that to you. When you least expect a source of inspiration to appear is when it often does.

For the first hour, my heart was heavy with thoughts about Pasang, but then the dog started being very playful, so I moved on to new thoughts. I decided to name the dog Buddy because that's just what he was and at a time when I needed one.

During the morning hours, I would meet people on the trail and ask for directions. By noon, I had gone down one valley and climbed to the top of the next ridge, only to find another valley before me and still no Taplejung. *Does this place really exist, or am I dreaming?* I thought. I must have taken a wrong turn somewhere during my first day, or I would have been there by now. Everyone kept telling me I was on the right path, but according to my map, I should have been in Taplejung yesterday at the latest.

Climbing the last ridge had done my feet in once again. To make matters worse, I was wearing new blisters where old ones had still not healed. As I rounded a curve in the trail, I saw an amazing number of marigolds on the hillside, so I wasn't paying much attention to what was ahead of me when suddenly, some children burst out of the bushes laughing, and they startled me. They had a chai stand set up and were selling to people on the trail. They were quite cute. The chai was on a small wooden table with a bench wide enough for only two people to sit down. The metal pitcher steamed with the fragrance of cinnamon, and I couldn't resist purchasing a cup.

The children got very excited when they spotted me; they began waving, jumping up and down, and saying something in Nepalese that I didn't understand.

When they spotted Buddy, they became a little afraid, backed up a little, and got quiet. He and I obviously weren't what they had expected. I sat down on the bench after taking my pack off. Buddy sat beside me and just panted softly; after all, he had been playing pretty hard.

I smiled at the children, took out my money, and they instantly understood. None of them spoke English, but the universal language of commerce came through loud and clear. The price was two rupees for a cup of chai, so I pulled out two one-rupee bills and laid them on the table. The little girl who seemed to be in charge reached out, took them, and giggled, which made the other three do the same. I think I was their first customer. Maybe I was their first paying customer; I wasn't sure. The other children included two more girls and a little brother to one of them. He obviously had not attained the normal male stature, so he was not listened to.

I took out a Clif bar, tore off some for Buddy, and then sat and ate the rest. As I ate and watched the children, I had a childhood memory surface that I hadn't thought of in years.

When I was ten, my parents and I took a summer vacation to visit relatives in Iowa and Minnesota. While in Minnesota, I was playing with some cousins in a hay barn. We had climbed high up on the stacks of hay bales and were swinging like Tarzan (my hero at that time). There were about twenty-five feet between the two stacks, and the rope was tied to the rafters in between. I was going to run from one end, grab the rope, and swing to the other side, but I missed the rope and fell about twenty feet to the dirt floor below.

I broke my left arm just up from the wrist, and my parents had to take me to the local hospital for treatment. When we got back home, my summer was pretty much lost. Consequently, on those deliciously warm summer days, Mom would make popsicles and I would sell them by the side of the street next to our house. I grew up in a "company" town that only had about 250 residents. In this case, the company was a Du Pont dynamite factory, and my dad was a foreman at the plant. Everyone knew everyone else and everybody's business—typical for a small town. All the kids grew up together, pretty much from birth through high school.

I had a lot of business at my Popsicle stand, between the kids and some of the parents stopping by. I don't remember how much I charged, but I knew it didn't matter; it was just a fun thing to do that brought all my friends around when I couldn't do much in the way of play. Little things like that made childhood exciting, even if you were temporarily sidelined with an injury. The guys thought the cast was cool, and the girls marveled at the story of being brave, playing Tarzan, and swinging on a rope up so high. Ah, to be a kid again, huh?

The chai tasted and smelled great, and since it was hot, I knew it wasn't likely going to make me sick. While sitting there, I started to teach Buddy to fetch a stick. I found one that he could play tug with, and then I threw it. The kids wanted to go and retrieve it, but I got them to understand what I was doing, so they just sat quietly and watched. I don't think they had ever seen someone teach a dog to do tricks. Pretty soon, Buddy caught on, and boy, did he enjoy this new game. I'd throw the stick about twenty yards, and he'd run as fast as he could to get to it, and in a cloud of dust, come to a halt. Then he would pick up the stick and run back to me with his ears lying flat against his head, saliva streaming from his grinning mouth. He would slide to another dusty halt, offering me the stick for another round.

I did this for about fifteen minutes until he was tuckered out and sat down to rest. The kids sold me one more chai before I realized it was time to get moving again. I had re-bandaged a couple of blisters and put on new moleskin so my feet could make it to wherever I stopped for dinner, which I hoped would be in Taplejung.

I was determined not let my sore feet ruin my adventure and kept pushing through the pain. *Resilience is key*, I thought to myself, *must be resilient!* After many years of long distance cycling, I had learned how to set pain aside in my mind and keep going. Having the tenacity to get beyond challenges in life is something we all deal with and learning how to handle them well is essential to success and happiness.

I waved goodbye to the children and headed out. Another ridge was before me, and it was going to take all afternoon to climb it. I could see the trail cresting the ridge next to an enormous tree, so at least I knew where I was going—well, sort of. It was about one-thirty in the afternoon, and the temperature was in the upper seventies. The sky was perfectly clear, and there was no breeze at all. *Another perfect day in paradise*, I thought. The air smelled like a botanical garden, full of moist sweetness and, at the same time, the smell of decaying leaves.

I had been climbing steadily for about an hour when I came across one of the trailside waterspouts that I found often. Since I was almost out of water, I stopped and took my pack off to rest for a few minutes. The view of the valley below was fantastic. The haze of morning had burned off, and I could see about fifty miles. One ridge gave way to another lower one and so on and so on. Each ridge was a slightly lighter color than the one before it. Overall, it looked more like a painting than the real thing.

Hoping to make the ridge top before three-thirty, I pressed on, forcing my feet to take more punishment than the Army had put them through during my basic training years earlier. It's funny the things you think about when you are trekking; you have no one to talk to, and you're just huffing and puffing along. Your mind wanders to the memories of past events, and you also speculate on what the future is going to bring. The nice thing about this experience is that you move into a different reality, mentally and physically, so you don't feel the physical pain you are experiencing.

> I WAS DETERMINED NOT LET MY SORE FEET RUIN MY ADVENTURE AND KEPT PUSHING THROUGH THE PAIN. RESILIENCE IS KEY, I THOUGHT TO MYSELF, MUST BE RESILIENT! AFTER MANY YEARS OF LONG DISTANCE CYCLING, I HAD LEARNED HOW TO SET PAIN ASIDE IN MY MIND AND KEEP GOING. HAVING THE TENACITY TO GET BEYOND CHALLENGES IN LIFE IS SOMETHING WE ALL DEAL WITH AND LEARNING HOW TO HANDLE THEM WELL IS ESSENTIAL TO SUCCESS AND HAPPINESS.

My friend Pete had taught me about how to move into this different reality when I was trying desperately to remove the pain of a lost love from my heart. He offered that if I would allow myself to wander to a far-off memory or think deeply about some subject during my long-distance cycling or mountain climbing, I could experience a state of mind in which I didn't feel any pain. I had tried this on several long bike rides that spanned 150 to 300 miles and discovered that it did work.

The Army memory suddenly took me back to basic training at Fort Lewis, Washington, in the winter of 1969. In the middle of a good night's sleep, our drill sergeant had awakened the platoon.

He was shouting orders to fall out and prepare for a forced march. It was about two o'clock, and the element of surprise was on his side. Our platoon got dressed in thermal underwear, fatigues, rain gear, and ponchos. Under the poncho was a pack with about thirty pounds of other Army-guy stuff. And, of course, last but not least, the metal helmet and M-14 rifle. I only weighed about 135 pounds in those days, so all my gear just about doubled my weight.

We marched in the rain until we arrived at our bivouac location. We erected our tents, dug rain trenches around them, ate breakfast, had rifle training at a shooting range, ate lunch, slogged through an obstacle course under live fire, and then dined on cold c-rations for dinner—followed by two hours of guard duty in the rain. All in all, a tough day.

Another forced march back to the fort was laid on us at two-thirty the next morning. Naturally, we were all exhausted and frustrated.

Marching us at a fast pace, the drill sergeant was attempting to beat the other platoons back, and when the fort came into sight, he ordered a double-time pace. Guys started dropping like flies. I got so angry with him that I loudly started calling him every bad name I could think of. He heard me and came to my side of the platoon. We were singing one of those stupid songs that made you learn to keep a proper cadence. Running beside me in the mud and rain, he asked me what my problem was, and I told him, "It is you, sir!"

"What did you call me, Renninson?" he shouted.

I don't want to repeat it here, but I told him just what I thought of him.

"That's what I thought you said," he replied, "and you know what, Renninson?"

"No, what, sir?"

"You're absolutely correct, so keep on running soldier," he said, grinning evilly.

He didn't have to wear all the gear we did so he could run very easily, plus he was obviously in great condition. When he smiled and ran ahead of me to the front of the platoon, the whole thing made sense. As soldiers, we needed to learn to take orders no matter what the circumstances and trust our commanders. I was a lot stronger when I arrived in Vietnam because of this training.

So here I was trudging up this very long mountain, and memories of the past allowed my mind to be somewhere else and ease my physical pain. I love my mind, the things it's capable of, and watching it work. It's not always positive; quite often, it is negative, so I must work hard to bring it back to the positive.

At 3:45 p.m., I crested the ridge, and once again, no Taplejung in sight. I was hot, tired, dirty, and hungry, and I was beginning to wonder whether I was meant to get to my destination.

On the top of many of the ridges, I would often find benches that had been built by the locals. They could sit and rest for a while after the long climb with their goods on their backs. This, thankfully, was one of those ridges. I sat down on the bench without taking my pack off and just leaned back against it. To my left, I could see the beautiful green valley ahead of me, and to my right, I could see the path and valley I had just come from. I laid my head back on the top of my pack and closed my eyes.

God, I thought to myself, *I have been three days trying to find this town, and I don't know which way to go or what to do, so I'm giving it to you. I've had it. I'm tired, and I ask you to show me the way.*

I took a deep breath, planning to rest a while before continuing. A few minutes later, having almost fallen asleep, I heard voices coming up the path to my right. Rolling my head ever so slightly to the right, I opened my right eye to see who was coming. Three very tough-looking young men in tattered and somewhat dirty clothing were approaching me.

"This is not what I had in mind," I said to God.

I closed my eyes and waited. As they approached me, they became quiet. Stopping a few feet from me, they whispered to one another. Then one of them came closer and said, "Are you okay?"

I opened my eyes and rolled my head toward him to see him better. "You speak English," I said.

"Yes, I do. But you have not answered my question; are you okay?"

I sat up with some difficulty and laughed, "Yes, besides being somewhat lost, I'm just fine."

His friends asked what I had said, and after his translation, they laughed also. He asked what I was doing there and where I was going; over the next few minutes, I shared my story with them, and they began to talk among themselves. After a few minutes, he turned to me and replied, "We are going to Taplejung, and you are welcome to join us."

"Wow, thank you! I would appreciate that very much," I said enthusiastically.

WHILE I WAS WRITING MY FIRST BOOK IN 1994, FREQUENTLY DURING THE NIGHT, I WOULD AWAKEN WITH A POEM IN MY MIND. HERE'S ONE OF THEM: "IN THE DARK QUIET OF THE NIGHT WHEN THE MIND IS RESTLESS WITH ANTICIPATION, ALL SEEMS POSSIBLE. SOMETIMES. SOMETIMES, IN THE DARK QUIET OF THE NIGHT, ALL IS RESTLESS WITH FEAR AND ANXIETY. STATE OF MIND AND THE DEGREE OF HAPPINESS THAT YOU ALLOW YOURSELF OFTEN DICTATE WHICH IS THE PREDOMINANT THEME. BUT NO MATTER HOW YOU LOOK AT IT, IN THE DARK QUIET OF THE NIGHT, THE MIND IS AN EXCITING PLACE TO RESIDE AND WATCH. SOMETIMES."

They started off down the trail at a brisk pace, and I got up to follow. Because of my feet, I couldn't keep up with them and rapidly fell behind. A short time later, as I rounded a bend and came to a "Y" in the trail, they were sitting there, waiting for me. I removed my pack, took out a couple of Clif bars and my water, and proceeded to eat. As they sat and watched me, I offered them some of the bars, but they didn't know what they were. After I had explained that to them, they tried the food very reluctantly.

"This is very good," said the one I had spoken to as he handed the remains to the others, who took tiny bites. They must have found the bars acceptable since they ate more readily. The food seemed to open them up to me, and they treated me in a friendlier manner. They talked for a few minutes among themselves. Then the fellow I could converse with turned to me and said, "You have a very heavy load and can't walk as fast as us. We could go that way," he said pointing down the path to the left, "or we can go this way and be to my friend's sister's farm in one hour, but it is much more okali (steep)."

"I think we should go the shorter way, even though it is steeper," I replied. "Thank you for helping me."

"We consider you to be a guest in our country, so we will do our best to help you."

"Will there be any place to eat along the way? I have only been eating my bars and need a regular meal."

"Yes, there is a small place at the top of the second ridge; we can stop there for some noodles."

His name was Pheriberi; he was twenty-six, and he and his friends were school inspectors. They traveled each week to the neighboring valleys and made sure the old buildings were safe for the children, repairing them if necessary. They had been out for three days and were on their way home. Needing to report for work the next morning, they were going out of their way to help me.

As we began walking again, I heard the two out in front yelling something. Not knowing what was going on, I hurried to catch up. There stood all three of the men, laughing and hollering something in Nepalese. Much to my surprise, we had reached one of those magical places where echoes of your voice would repeat down a canyon very clearly and distinctly.

It was fun. I enjoyed a couple of hollers myself. Each time, we would all laugh together. Life's small pleasures delight at any age, no matter where you are. These men knew how to enjoy life and laugh. It was very pleasant to have some people to travel with who enjoyed themselves along the way.

When these three men walked into my life, I was not too sure that God had heard my request for help. They appeared rough and tough, and I felt uneasy, but then I found that they were the perfect group to come along and assist me. I had sunk to instant judgment based on their appearance, and now I felt embarrassed. I silently thanked God for the lesson and smiled at how things never are what they appear to be. I should have known I would be taken care of and just accept what came along, but trust is not a mind thing; it's a heart thing. We are so conditioned to listen to our minds that we often overlook the true feeling of faith that's screaming to be heard.

Halfway up a steep ridge, Pheriberi gave me his bamboo walking stick. He could see that I was struggling to keep my footing on the rough gravel trail. It helped so much, and when I told him how I appreciated it, he beamed ear-to-ear. I was determined to be resilient and push through the pain; his gesture helped.

Just as it was starting to get dark, we crested the second ridge, and sure enough, there was a small, one room, trailside cafe. One of Pheriberi's friends had gone ahead and arranged for the yum-yum noodles to be prepared. I was starved, and the hot broth rejuvenated me. I was getting cold, so it also warmed me. We all sat in the hut on the wooden benches next to the indoor fire. The smoke was very thick, and the only light was from the fire. The owner and his wife talked to my newfound friends and smiled very toothless grins my way. They were very hospitable and friendly. I paid the café owners, and we left.

Later, around six o'clock, we arrived at the destination where we would spend the night. I sat down on the front porch of the farmhouse and removed my boots. My feet were badly swollen, and it scared me when I took off the boots and saw my bloodstained socks. Altogether, I had twenty-two different blisters. What a mess. The children of the farm sat and watched as I cleaned and medicated my feet. The Merthiolate stung like the dickens, but I had to make sure the blisters were not getting infected.

I had noticed that Pheriberi and his friends had left earlier with the sister, and now, out of the darkness, they returned. "This farm doesn't have enough room for all four of us, so we are going to another house just behind this barn a short way," Pheriberi informed me.

Instead of putting my boots back on, I put on my rubber flip-flop sandals. That would prove to be a huge mistake. I stowed my gear away, got my pack on, and proceeded to follow them down the narrow dirt path along the barn and beyond. Having become accustomed to the stability of my boots, my feet felt weird, sliding back and forth on the rubber sandals. Therefore, I had to walk very carefully. I thought we were only going a short way and that wearing the flip-flops would be less painful than putting my socks and boots back on. Fortunately, it was a short distance. When we arrived at the next farmhouse, which sat on a terrace, there was a rock wall that we had to climb.

As is the case the world over in rural areas, whenever a rock wall is constructed, rocks are laid in such a manner that they create a staircase sticking out of the wall. I had my walking stick in one hand and my flashlight in the other as I proceeded to step up on the protruding stone. I stepped up on the first rock with my right foot, and as I raised my left foot up, I hit the edge of the step with the outside of my big toe. In the sandal, the toe was totally unprotected. As pain shot through my body, I knew I had done some serious damage. I gritted my teeth and kept the upward momentum going. I hobbled the thirty feet to the front porch of the farmhouse, where a kerosene lantern was burning. Seeing a bench that I could sit on, I moved quickly toward it, and the two men occupying it got up and moved out of my way.

I removed my pack and untied the top compartment containing a first-aid kit. Then I sat down before looking at my foot. As I brought my foot up to rest on my right knee, those present uttered a collective gasp. A small geyser of blood was spurting out of the toe; most of the skin was ripped back, revealing muscle and inner tissue. I panicked a bit when I saw what I had done to myself. Knowing that I had to stop the bleeding, I took the piece of skin that had been ripped back and replaced it over the gaping hole.

I took one of my bandanas, wrapped it around the toe, and compressed the cloth against the toe with as much pressure as I could stand. I hoped this would eventually stop the bleeding.

I couldn't help myself; I vomited from fear and pain.

Suddenly, the front porch was full of people: the farmer, his wife, their three sons, the three men I had arrived with, and four workers. They all sat or stood and watched, murmuring to one another, eyes wide with amazement and curiosity. I was feeling cold, so with my free hand, I took out my jacket and a cap from my pack. After a few moments, I was feeling a little better; I didn't go into shock, but I knew I had been close.

When I felt enough time had elapsed, I removed the bandana. The bleeding had stopped, and the three-sided piece of torn skin had reattached itself almost perfectly. I knew what the next step needed to be, and I wasn't looking forward to it at all. I opened the first-aid kit and removed the Motel 6 sewing kit. I threaded a needle and took a deep breath. As I eased the needle into the ragged edge of the tear, my toe jerked uncontrollably.

Looking up at Pheriberi, his eyes wide and mouth open, I said,

"Pheriberi, I need your help. Will you please hold my foot steady?"

He didn't say anything; he just knelt in front of me and gently took my foot in his dark, warm hands. His touch was so comforting that I felt strengthened by the simple act. I ran the first stitch, tugged it snuggly into place and proceeded to do four more. By the time I was finished, I was sick to my stomach and felt drained and weak. Since the bleeding had stopped, and my toe was throbbing like crazy, I took two ibuprofen tablets. Then I lay back on the bench and put my foot up on the window ledge to elevate it and slow the throbbing.

I had rested only a few minutes with my eyes closed when Pheriberi said to me, "You can eat now. Come, and I will wash your hands." He helped me to my feet after I had slipped on my sandals. We walked unsteadily to the edge of the porch, where he poured water from a pitcher over my bloodstained fingers. The cool water felt good, and so did the sensation of being clean.

He assisted me into the farmhouse, where we sat on the adobe-like floor in front of the fire. It was now very dark, and the only light was that of the cooking fire and kerosene lantern. The farmer's wife had been preparing dahl baht, boiled cauliflower, broccoli, and rice. As she handed me a metal tray and proceeded to place food on it, I noticed that the other individuals were standing in the doorway, watching. Since I was the guest, they would eat after I did. This made me feel bad because they had put in a hard day of work and were undoubtedly very hungry.

In typical Nepali fashion, I had to eat with my right hand and not use any utensils. Some of the food was cold since they had no way to keep one course warm while another is cooked. My stomach was queasy at best from my self-induced injury, and I couldn't eat very much. I knew that this would insult the farmer's wife, but I had no stomach for the bland, mostly cold food. I ate as much as I could, and then I told Pheriberi that I was not feeling well and was very tired. He understood, but I know the lady of the house felt slighted.

The farmer's eldest son took me to the side of the hut where they had prepared a bench for me to sleep on. It was about four feet off the ground. When I laid down, it was a foot short of being long enough for my 5' 10" frame. Near my head was a doorway that led to the boys' room. On the other side was a bamboo fence that acted as a bullpen. The roof was low, so I had to bend over slightly. The bull's pungent odor didn't help my upset stomach.

My foot was killing me; I knew I had better check on it. I rolled out my sleeping bag for a soft place to sit and re-bandaged my toe. It was oozing a clear fluid, but it wasn't bleeding. The Advil had done the job, and it didn't throb nearly as much, but it was quite swollen. I rolled up my jacket and placed it under my foot to elevate it somewhat. That only took a few minutes, I'm sure, but it seemed like hours. As I lay down to prepare to sleep, the boys of the house finished their dinner and came to talk to me.

Bhawani Prasad Niraula, the eldest son, was seventeen or eighteen. He was well-educated and spoke almost perfect English. After completing the local schooling, he was going to Kathmandu University. We spoke for almost two hours until I couldn't hold my eyes open any longer. His greatest joy was to use his skills in English with someone who spoke it all the time. He asked for help in using the right words. Then he translated for the other boys and workers gathered around in the light of a kerosene lantern. By now, the night air had gotten cold, so I added another shirt and my stocking cap.

The farmer's wife brought me chai, which warmed me and tasted exceedingly good. I smiled at her in appreciation, but she showed no sign of acknowledgment, only performing the duties of the household.

When I could snuggle down into my sleeping bag and try to sleep, I found it difficult to get comfortable. My foot hurt, and the table was hard and unforgiving. I didn't get much sleep and almost welcomed the sunrise.

TAPLEJUNG AT LAST

In the morning, while I was still in my sleeping bag, Pheriberi sat down next to me. "Are you feeling better?" he asked.

"I'm still tired. My foot is throbbing," I replied, yawning.

"Would you like tea?"

"Yes, I would. Thank you."

He came back in a few minutes with chapati and tea. I sat eating in my sleeping bag and watched the household activities around me. It was a cold morning, so I didn't want to leave my warm, synthetic cocoon.

"We must leave soon," Pheriberi said as he watched me finish my tea. "We were going to Taplejung last night, but we believed staying with you was a better thing to do. Now we will be late for our jobs if we do not start soon."

"I am sorry if I am causing you a problem, but I have really appreciated your help. I will get ready as fast as I can."

It took me about fifteen minutes to get dressed, pack my gear, and say goodbye to the family. The mother would not say anything to me; as I had surmised, she felt insulted from the night before. I told Bhawani to thank her for her hospitality and wish her well, but she still did not respond. I felt bad, but what could I do? I couldn't leave any money because that would have insulted her further, so I sat down to put on my boots. This proved to be extremely painful. My injured toe was very swollen and oozing. I re-bandaged it quickly and put on clean socks. I loosened the shoestrings as far as I could, and I still had to force my foot into the cold, stiff boot. The pain made me sick to my stomach, a little dizzy, and caused me to break out in a sweat. I tied the boot up as tightly as I could and stood up, feeling wobbly. The walking stick that Pheriberi had provided helped me keep my balance. My feet warmed up through simple movement, but I walked like a ninety-year-old man.

About thirty minutes later, I caught up to Pheriberi and his two friends sitting beside the path. "We can't wait for you today," he said sadly. "We must leave you now and hurry on. As you can see, the path continues around the valley. See where it comes out on the other side?" he said, pointing to a spot about four miles away across the horseshoe-shaped valley. "Keep looking for that place two more times as you round the next valleys, and you should be in Taplejung mid-day."

"I can't tell you how much I thank you," I said as I stood leaning on his walking stick.

"Maybe we will see each other in Taplejung; if not, have a good life. Namaste."

"Namaste," I said to him and each of his friends. They took off at a brisk pace down the trail, turning to wave and holler Namaste again.

The sun peeked over the ridge behind me, and the cool morning air was clear and clean. The brilliance of the green of the foliage in the mornings always took my breath away; it was beautiful and smelled wonderful, like a freshly cut lawn but different. The mornings also brought the songs of the many birds high up in the trees, greeting the day. Through the forest, I could see the trio of men as they hurried along the path about a mile ahead of me.

"Thank you, God, for the people you keep bringing to help me on my journey. Even with the pain in my feet, I am still having a great adventure and a lot of fun. Give me safe passage again today, and keep my foot from getting infected."

It had become a habit of mine to talk to God throughout my life.

When I was in Vietnam during the war, I had done so frequently, as you might expect. I never lost the desire to talk to God whenever I was happy or sad. *Knowing* that I was in good hands, I took off walking for the fourth day. I now knew that I would be in Taplejung sometime later that day.

The trail had some up and down spots as I had come to expect, but I didn't expect the numerous waterfalls that started to appear. On my trip to Annapurna, they had been frequent, but they hadn't been on this trip. Now, as I was getting higher into the Himalayas, water was everywhere. Consequently, the falls popped up out of nowhere. Some were small—only eight or ten feet—while others fell several hundred feet into mist-shrouded pools surrounded by verdant plant life and tall, very old trees.

As I was preparing to leave Bhawani's home, I had asked him whether he would like to keep Buddy. I had known I was going to get attached to him. However, he and the boys seemed to like each other. Buddy had become accustomed to love and attention in the few short days with me, so I needed to leave him somewhere he would continue to get great care. I had noticed that he and the boys had played a lot during the time I was at their home. Bhawani was thrilled at the prospect and immediately said yes. I knew Buddy had found a good home, and the boys would pay attention to him, but now I missed him scurrying around. Sometimes, it's harder to say goodbye to animals than it is to some human beings. I had given him a hug as I left, and he seemed to know he was to stay. He sat on the front porch and quietly watched me leave. I didn't look back.

Walking along thinking about Buddy, another memory surfaced that I hadn't thought of in years. After returning home from Vietnam, I had gone to work for a company that managed different businesses. One of my jobs was to manage the weigh scales at a rock quarry south of Colorado Springs. I was living in a deserted restaurant without electricity, but there was running water, a fireplace, and a gas stove—generally, it wasn't bad. I hadn't really gotten used to being back home and being around a lot of people anyway, so the time alone was almost welcome.

As I weighed the dump trucks coming and going, the day could sometimes drag along. I had taken the assignment in late spring, so it would occasionally snow and then be warm for a day or so. On one of the warm days, I noticed a dog lying among the trees on the quarry's edge about one hundred yards away. I asked one of the truckers I had gotten to know whether he would pick up a two-sided dog dish and a bag of dog food for me. Later in the afternoon, when he returned with the supplies, I placed the food and water halfway between the dog and me.

Sure enough, about thirty minutes later, I watched as the dog slowly meandered toward the bowl. It was a black and white Border Collie, weighing about twenty-five pounds. I could see that he was skinny and his coat was full of burrs.

On the third day, I coaxed him to me, petted him, and fed him at the doorway to my hut. Once he let go of his fear of me and allowed me to brush him and clean him up, we were good friends. I named him Hamilton, and he remained a loyal and wonderful friend for the next eleven years.

After my wife and I had moved into a new home, Hamilton became ill. He couldn't stand or walk. I took him to a host of veterinarians to find out what was wrong with him. Most of his problems stemmed from old age, but he also had some internal problems that were incurable. When I left for work one morning, I laid him in a sunny spot on the floor because he liked being in the sun. Returning home that night, I found him in the same spot, panting and smiling his silly grin and wagging his tail, happy to see me.

I knelt beside him and started to cry out loud. He must have thought that I wanted to sing, so he started to howl with me. I cried even harder. I hugged him, talked with him for a while, and then took him to the vet where he was put to sleep an hour later. God, that was awful. And leaving Buddy wasn't easy either. I had learned that I get attached to dogs and cats so easily that I must remain somewhat detached or I have a really hard time leaving them.

I feel we can open up to animals easily because they depend on us so much. They love us unconditionally and are so inherently happy that we can't help but get attached to them. I sometimes think that because they can't talk, it makes it easier to love them and harder to say goodbye. I have only had one animal since, and I don't think I will have another, at least not for a long while. This memory had brought tears to my eyes and slowed my pace, so I stopped to enjoy the scenery and eat something.

As I sat and journaled, I realized how these surfacing memories were having a cleansing effect on me. The spiritual nature of remembering and releasing old, painful memories made them less difficult to endure as time passed. They were still "my" memories, but no longer did they have the paralyzing effect they had often had in the past.

A few years ago, after I had gone through a divorce, a friend of mine introduced me to the cathartic experience of working with my inner child. Many people feel that they have had bad things happen to them as children, either through real or imagined traumas.

By bringing them up from their deep hiding places, facing them, and forgiving the people involved, they can essentially "forgive and forget" and move on with their lives. The spiritual nature of this trek was doing the same thing for me, and for the most part, I was grateful for it.

I took a deep breath, closed my eyes, and meditated for about fifteen minutes. I realized that this was one of those wondrous moments when I was truly happy with my life, whom I had become, and where I was going.

With my eyes closed, I breathed the clean, warm mountain air and listened to the breeze rustle through the leaves of the plants and trees. I could hear the birds, the buzzing of the insects, and the sound of my own heart beating. The thought passed through my mind that no one else was experiencing what I was at that moment. I was the center of my universe. My experiences were mine and no one else's. Despite all the beings on this planet, and who knows how many on other planets in who knows how many other galaxies, no one else was me. As small as that makes you feel, it also makes you feel very special because you are the only one with your mind, physical makeup, personality, traits, and desires.

My meditations took many forms; sometimes I was just quiet, with minimal mental activity, and other times I let my mind flow with the cosmos. Being in "flow" was my favorite state because I would receive wonderful thoughts that stretched my imagination. Sometimes, while in times of struggle, I would pray during meditation for guidance and strength. These times of contemplation gave me insight into how I felt about issues that were down deep in my subconscious and helped me resolve those issues to further my growth. Learning to be alone is hard for most people, but if you can be alone with your soul, you're not alone at all. In fact, that is probably the best company to be in whenever possible.

As I opened my eyes and looked at the snow-capped peaks of the Himalayas in the distance, I felt my own spirituality, my own oneness with God, had never been so close. Never had this connection been more intense and intimate, nor more loving and wonderful. This kind of *knowing* can only come with the opportunity to be with one's self on a spiritual plane that allows no other type of thought to enter. I had come to this magical little country knowing that I was in store for a great adventure, which held the opportunity to explore who I was and how I fit in the overall scheme of things.

I wasn't quite sure that I would ever totally understand how I fit, but the exploration was certainly exciting. My poem of "the mind being an exciting place to be in the dark of the night" was proving to be just as thrilling in broad daylight.

I rose and started walking with resilient energy and determination to reach Taplejung. I had walked for only a few moments when I heard the sounds of a busy marketplace emanating from over a small, green knoll. As I reached the top and gazed upon the small valley below, I saw Taplejung. Feeling elated, I did a little jig and laughed out loud.

It was Saturday, and the marketplace on the edge of town was busy with people hurrying to buy and sell. There must have been several hundred-people sitting in what looked like a flea market. There were narrow aisles between small tents or lean-tos that housed farmers and craftsmen, all hocking their wares in a noisy and festive atmosphere. The hillside next to the market was green and covered with colorful wildflowers. Off in the distance, massive Kanchenjunga was looking down on me from over 28,000 feet. It was my first view of the mountain since flying into Badraphur. It loomed high and lofty in the clear, noonday sun, without a cloud to obscure the view. It had taken me seven hours to reach Taplejung from Bhawani's farm, and I was very happy to be here and see the beauty ahead of me.

As I eased my way through the market, I attracted much attention. I was about a foot and a half taller than anyone else there, with my big, green backpack and orange bandana. Little kids followed me, pointing and giggling. The adults looked at me with curiosity and wonder. All of them talked and laughed and then waved to me as I waved back and said "Namaste" to them. My wristwatch and cameras seemed to draw as much attention as anything. The preset alarm on my watch beeped on the hour. I had preset it often so I would remember to wait until my iodine tablets had dissolved and done their magic on the local water. When it sounded, the children became quiet so they could listen to it, and when it stopped, they would look at each other and laugh.

> MY MEDITATIONS TOOK MANY FORMS; SOMETIMES I WAS JUST QUIET, WITH MINIMAL MENTAL ACTIVITY, AND OTHER TIMES I LET MY MIND FLOW WITH THE COSMOS. BEING IN "FLOW" WAS MY FAVORITE STATE BECAUSE I WOULD RECEIVE WONDERFUL THOUGHTS THAT STRETCHED MY IMAGINATION.

Everyone was dressed in his or her "Sunday best," as we used to say back home. The women were especially colorful in their bright, handmade clothing in yellows, reds, oranges, and blues that made the whole scene look like a carnival, with each face smiling and happy. Earrings and nose rings were the norm on the women but not the men. It made me laugh when I thought how new and original kids back home felt they were with their piercing and tattooing. It has been the custom here and around the world for centuries. At home, it was a fad; here, it is the culture.

I was hot, tired, and tiring of iodine flavored water I wanted the safety of a beer, so I stopped at the first teahouse that I came to on the edge of the town. There I met the only Yuppie Nepali I hope I ever meet. His name was Dezandra, but I called him Zandra for short, and he was from Kathmandu. He spoke some English, wore

Army style clothing, dark glasses, a Walkman, etc., etc. He was very proud of the western style dress and mannerisms that were his style. I had to laugh at his pretentious nature because he looked so out of place with his own people. As I sat and tended to my blisters, he informed me that he was a very famous guide in this area, and he would like to introduce me to his two trekkers from "Sudan."

I wasn't all that interested in meeting his clients, but I needed to find a restaurant and get some real food, and he was mildly entertaining, so I let him give me a tour of Taplejung. This was one of the few times in Nepal that I saw cobblestone streets. They were in terrible shape and deteriorating from lack of attention. Taplejung was typically poor and rundown. The narrow streets were lined with shops of the usual sort: clothing, brass pots and pans, woven baskets, and small restaurants. Most of the buildings had two stories and looked to be well over one hundred years old. The shopkeepers lived in quarters on the second floor.

We walked for a while until my feet began to hurt too much, then we stopped at a small cafe for chai. While Zandra ordered for both of us in his pretentious and boisterous manner, his "Sudanese" clients heard him from the street and came in. Much to my surprise and delight, they weren't Sudanese, but Swedish. Jon was twenty-two and Janos twenty-one. They were both tall, blond, and friendly. I think they were almost happier than I to find someone who could speak English and was from the Western world.

The three of us hit it off almost immediately, telling horror stories of the trek to Taplejung since they had been trying to find the town for two days. It made me feel a little better about my own navigation problems. Their main concern was that Zandra was taking advantage of them financially. Since they didn't speak any Nepalese, they weren't sure whether they were paying the right amount for food or rooms. Zandra would tell them how much he needed to pay innkeepers, and they would give him the money. This was a problem that we tackled together over the next few days.

"I really don't want to trek back to Cavalli, and I noticed on my map that there is supposed to be an airport near here," I said to them over our chai.

"You mean that we could fly back to Kathmandu?" Jon asked.

"I think the flight takes you to Badraphur, where you can get a bus or a connecting flight to Kathmandu."

"Well, if that doesn't work, we have also heard from Zandra that there is a road to Cavalli, so maybe we could get a ride on a truck," Janos replied.

"Yeah, I had heard about the road too, but I never saw it; did you?" I asked.

"No, we didn't see it, but we did see the trucks here in town. Why don't we try to find the airline office, if there is one, and then plan from there?" Jon said.

In agreement, we set out to find the Royal Nepal Airline office. As we walked along, I kept an eye open for Pheriberi as well, hoping that he could aid in a translation that we could trust. After about an hour, we located the airline office, only to find that the flights were booked for the next three weeks. It was only a twelve-seat plane that flew once a day if the weather was good. We decided to go back to the teahouse on the edge of town where I had met Zandra to get a room for the night and have lunch. It was then I realized it was almost four o'clock, and I still hadn't eaten.

As the three of us relaxed and talked, I got their story. Both were college students, and they had taken six months off to see the world. They had been on the road for two months and traveled through Iran, Pakistan, India, and now Nepal. Thus far, they had been in a terrible bus accident, in a severe rainstorm, had several bouts of diarrhea, and met some horrible guides. They considered it all an adventure and were quite pleased with their experience.

Though I was considerably older than they were (although I feel twenty-eight most of the time anyway), we got along quite well and seemed to have a lot to talk about. As the next few days unfolded,

I took on the role of a mature protector, sage, and mentor wrapped up in one. This was a nice, but different, experience for me.

Since I had been to Nepal before and had had a wonderful guide in Tashi Lama, I knew the difference between a good a guide and a bad one. The one they had was bad; I told them how to deal with him and not to take any of his double-talk. I told them how to check the prices of things and how to ask him questions that he had to answer truthfully. It took a little time, but they learned.

We sat in the little restaurant on the main floor of the teahouse and ordered yum-yum noodles and a beer. I gave Zandra a few orders for the boys, and he started to learn that I wasn't a novice trekker. I acquired his respect over time, but at first, he was reluctant to relinquish the control he had established.

Our food finally arrived, and after eating, we went to the room we had rented for the night, unpacked, and took a nap. It's amazing how this type of travel wears you out.

Our room came with four cots and enough space for all our gear. As I slowly fell asleep, I felt good about having arrived in Taplejung. Having met some wonderful people to share my trek with, I felt confident that we would be able to help each other. To what extent I didn't know, but I had a feeling that we were going to share something special. We napped for only an hour, and then one by one, we rose and took care of personal stuff.

"I think I have something that will help your blisters greatly," Janos said while rummaging through his backpack. "Yeah, here it is."

He handed me a small, flat, cellophane package that was about three inches square and filled with a flesh-colored substance. It was a medicated bandage and worked on the principle of heat. Once pressed into place and wrapped with an ace bandage or tape, the warmth of your skin melted the cellophane and bonded the medicated pad to you. It created a second skin that both medicated and cushioned. It felt wonderful, and I didn't think it would come off in my boot like the Band-Aids I had been using. I used one on each heel and on my stitched big toe. I could walk again. My feet were so sore that I still had some difficulty, but it was far better than before.

During the rest of the late afternoon, we sat in the room, cleaned our gear, traded film and medical supplies, shared our stories of being on the road, and just got to know each other. By dinnertime, we had formed a good relationship. They laughed a lot and kidded me, and I returned the favor. When the subject of security came up, I told them that I locked everything with a combination lock. I was surprised that they had never seen one before. I had brought two with me; I showed them how to work one and gave it to them. They seemed genuinely grateful.

We took our time looking for a restaurant that had a menu we liked. Walking with the new patches helped me immensely as we journeyed around town. Over a dinner of dahl and rice, we discussed where to go in the next few days. I told them I only had five days until I had to get back to Badraphur for my flight to Kathmandu. I knew that once we made it to Cavalli, we would still be two days out. Therefore, I had three days to hike closer to Kanchenjunga.

The more we talked, the more everyone liked the idea of staying together, so we formulated a plan with Zandra to trek out a day and a half and then back to Taplejung. If we could arrange it, we would then hitch a ride on one of the Tata trucks to Cavalli. It sounded like fun, and even Zandra got caught up in the excitement. We shared a couple of beers to celebrate our newfound friendship, and then we headed back to the teahouse to get a good night's sleep.

LETTING GO

Taplejung had a garrison of Gurkhas to patrol the border area near Sikkim, India, and my comfort level was lower since my trekking permit territory had expired about fifty miles back. Luckily, each time I had encountered one of the Gurkhas, they never asked for my permit. After eating breakfast and packing, we left Taplejung, heading off toward Kanchenjunga. To leave town, we had to pass the Gurkha station. I smiled and waved to the guard on duty, and he nodded in their typically stoic manner. I felt relieved when we were safely out of sight. It felt good to be on the trail again, and my feet felt better, having received a well-deserved rest during the previous day.

I felt a renewed excitement trekking with new people, because of the company and the conversation. During dinner and before we had fallen asleep the night before, the three of us had spoken about all sorts of subjects. I was sure that today wasn't going to be any different.

"Janos, have you ever noticed that one of the biggest ills that befalls mankind is judgment?" I asked, wanting to talk about my favorite philosophical subjects. "No matter where you go, it seems that everyone has an axe to grind about someone. We, as human beings, can't seem to let go of the idea that we have the power to judge our peers. In America, during the sixties, our nation seemed to touch on the concept of a non-judgmental attitude. Although still prevalent, racial prejudices, religious dogma, and strict moral positions became lesser issues as my generation tried to instill the virtues of peace and love."

"The kids coming up today have been on that track too," Janos replied. "They are a couple of decades apart, but many are nonetheless non-judgmental in their attitudes toward issues like race, sexual preference, you know, stuff like that," Janos replied.

I couldn't help but be somewhat impressed with the level of maturity in these two. Being from Sweden, they provided me with insight into how another culture looked at this subject; plus, they seemed eager to share their thoughts.

"In Sweden, as with most Scandinavian and European countries, the majority seem to look at the world as a global community, rather than as individual countries. To be sure, we are proud of where we are from and have that competitive spirit, but having been brought up in the computer and Internet age, we look at the world as being much smaller and accepting than in older generations," Janos said.

In their travels, they had seen much racism, class differences, and prejudicial judgment, including the inhumane treatment of women in India, Iraq, and Iran. Until just recently, even in Nepal, housewives were not always allowed to go to school, something they often needed to do to better themselves, especially if their husbands were killed or injured in climbing accidents and they needed to feed their families. The spread of human rights throughout the world seemed to be moving at a snail's pace, but moving just the same. The conclusion of our discussions seemed to be that no human being had the right to impose any values or judgment on another human, no matter what the reason or excuse. Getting the older generations that have all the power to accept new ways of thinking and to discard old prejudices was an ongoing struggle that we all faced.

We all agreed that the little country of Nepal seemed to harbor the least of these prejudices, overall. Gender discrimination aside, most people accepted you as you appeared and for what you said, not for preconceived notions based on skin color, religion, or nationality. It is very idealistic to think that we all can overcome the urge to judge others completely, but we just should try, and it will make a difference.

At the end of the first day of trekking toward Kanchenjunga, we could finally see the mountain in all its majesty, soaring high above the foothills we were trekking through. Totally covered in the newly fallen snow, it appeared to stand out mysteriously against the green jungle environment.

I knew I wasn't going to get as close as I had originally planned, largely because of the few days I spent trying to find Taplejung.

During the early afternoon, we came across a group of Europeans who were on their way to summit Kanchenjunga; we trekked together for several hours and then camped next to each other. They had quite an entourage—seven porters, two cooks, and a guide. The three of us were amazed by how much food they had brought along. Luckily for our taste buds, they invited us to join them for dinner. Since they would be climbing in a few days, they were carbo-loading, and pasta was the meal of choice.

Two of them spoke some broken English, and my Swedish

friends spoke some German, which the other two spoke somewhat. Only I didn't speak any of the other languages, so I was relegated to sketchy translations or being left out entirely. That wasn't all that bad, since it gave me the opportunity to sit and watch the dynamics of the group.

Michael was the leader, and he came from the wealthiest family. At twenty-eight, he had a very mature presence and commanded the attention and respect of his fellow climbers. He was always barking orders to the porters, which I wasn't sure he did as much to keep them in line as to give himself an elevated position in front of everyone else.

Angelo had a big smile, a hearty laugh, and really enjoyed the vino. He was the oldest at thirty-three, but he didn't attempt to run the group at all. He was content to bring joy to anyone he talked to, and he was genuinely having the time of his life. He respected the Nepalese greatly and often made faces behind Michael when he was ordering them about. This always made the Nepali laugh.

Gino was the youngest, but I never found out his age; I would have guessed twenty-five. It was his first time away from home, and he was shy and somewhat quiet. He busied himself with his gear, but you could tell he was always very aware of what was going on around him. He would smile to himself at Angelo's antics. Once when I caught him smiling, he blushed; his innocence was refreshing and fun.

Joseph was the consummate traveler, having been in many countries and climbed for most of his thirty years. He would be considered the technically-correct climber and probably have the last word on how their climb would proceed once on the mountain. Since he spoke German, he talked with Jon and Janos the most.

Following Michael's instructions as best he could, the head cook prepared a wonderful meal of pasta with a mushroom marinara, garlic bread, and mandarin oranges for dessert. Several bottles of red wine made the rounds and then chai before we called it a night. I was very appreciative of the great meal since I hadn't had anything like that for over a week. As I crawled into my sleeping bag under the star-filled sky, I was satiated from the food as well as the entertainment of all who were present. What an international flair my trek had suddenly taken—Nepali, American, Swedish, Italian, and Austrian: all with the common goal of enjoying Nepal and everyone we met.

The day had been full of laughter, camaraderie, beautiful scenery, and the kind of freedom that you long for when you are immersed in everyday activities back home. As I fell asleep, I thanked God for feet that were healing, good weather, friendly trekkers to travel with, and peace of mind. It was in that peace of mind that my awareness had taken a quantum leap. More than ever before, I was aware of my multi-sensory abilities; to read people and situations clearly was intoxicating and appreciated. To be —without any other requirements —and to enjoy each day fully without fear: what more could you ask for? I was full of love for life as I lost consciousness— what a great feeling.

TOTAL STRANGERS

The day began much as the previous one had ended, with Angelo playing pranks and the rest of us trying not to get caught in one. It was great fun, even though I didn't understand half of what was being said. I vowed to learn a foreign language when I returned home, but which one does one select and why? So, of course, I never did it; it was perpetually postponed.

We had begun to attain some serious elevation, and by 10:00 a.m. we had reached a tundra-like landscape. It felt good to put on warm clothing as the temperature dropped. After all, I had brought all this high-altitude gear; if I had to carry it anyway, I might as well get to use it. I noticed that my breathing was coming harder and our pace had slowed, so I knew we were nearing the top of the pass. Around noon, we made the summit of the pass, and Kanchenjunga was in full view to the north. It was a very clear day, and the 360-degree view was spectacular.

The porters had gone ahead of us mid-morning and already established a lunch camp. Everyone knew we would return to Taplejung at this point, so we made the mid-day meal a special occasion. The attitude of the entire group had changed. We had become a little more somber. We sat together in a circle, eating and enjoying the vistas of snowcapped mountains. Kanchenjunga, now only a day and a half away, loomed very large; quiet with its beauty hiding its many dangers. The air was cold, and a small breeze was whipping the Hindu prayer flags that hung from a small stupa nearby.

After goodbyes, I stood at the top of the pristine mountain pass and watched the band of trekkers, climbers, and porters descend away from me; I felt a sense of loss. Only a day and a half had passed; still, we had shared so much. The sense of *knowing* that I had experienced this time for a reason was very strong. The hard part was trying to figure out what the reason was and why I needed to experience it in the first place. I know that each time I have felt this way, I have grown in some way that made me a better person.

Three years earlier, I had shared much love with a woman I'll call Janet, and at that moment, at the top of that mountain pass, I missed her greatly. Once again, as with Pasang, I wanted to share this experience with her. I know I am not alone in this life, but tied to some by blood, others by friendship and some by a deeper bond that never goes away. I had met other women and enjoyed good times with them, but my heart always went back to the same one who had pierced the inner, veiled depths of my being. Part of the reason I came to Nepal was to try to move on from her. I have a nasty habit of getting so involved that it takes me years to let go. I don't know whether that shows me the depth of the love I can have for someone or the depth of the pain it takes to get over it. It would be almost a year and a half later before she would once again re-enter my life with news that would be received with great happiness and sadness. But for the moment, I wanted to hold her and share my emotion.

So here I was, almost three years since we had abruptly stopped seeing each other, and I was still carrying a torch the size of a Cadillac, which was getting too heavy. It was too much, period. But I couldn't get rid of it. I would look for the metaphysical basis, but I couldn't find one. I knew that part of this trip was to find myself—for a lot of reasons, and this was one of them. I had been forcing myself to look at other women. I hated it. So here in the most spiritual place on earth, I kept waiting for that proverbial lightning bolt of realization to strike me in the forehead, so I'd know why she and I were so connected.

Why had she suddenly come rushing back to my consciousness? It wasn't just a little feeling of the loss of her; it was a big feeling. As I walked, I started to cry, and I hated this emotional weakness in myself. Unfortunately, I possessed the ability to come to tears far too easily—over sad movies, a moving passage in a book, funerals, weddings, the playing of "Taps" and "The Star-Spangled Banner"— emotional songs that are often shared with total strangers.

Total strangers—it seemed that my life was constantly filled with them. I revel in my ability to enjoy the experiences and the people. They always have something to teach you if you look for it. I sometimes feel closer to them than I do to people I've known for the entirety of my life. Total strangers will often tell you things they won't share with members of their own family or their intimate friends. It's that wonderful sense that you will never see that person again so you can share something that you need to without fear of how you will be judged or perceived. Most strangers just accept you and your story at face value and move on. No guilt, shame, anger, or sadness—just life being lived as best as it can. Mistakes, joys, and triumphs are all wrapped up in brief interludes.

This kind of atmosphere permeates trekking. As Jon, Janos, Zandra, and I turned and walked from the mountaintop, we were all quiet and stayed that way for the better part of an hour. We each allowed the events of the past two days to settle into our collective memories for recollection at a future date when we each would tell the story in our own way to another stranger—a stranger who would listen, learn and leave, possibly to share it with someone else someday.

The air became warmer, and clothing started to be shed until we were back to our jungle attire, sweat-soaked and dirty.

The Himalayas were all the shades of green one could imagine as we arrived at the place where we had spent the previous night. Jon went about setting up camp with Zandra, while Janos and I climbed to the top of the nearest hill to shoot some photos.

"What is bothering you so much today?" he asked me.

"I have been feeling the loss of a woman I stopped seeing three years ago," I replied. "Have you ever been so in love that you couldn't let go of the feeling for years?"

"Well, obviously, being a little younger than you, I haven't had time for many of those things to have occurred. But, yes, to answer your question, I, to a lesser degree, have experienced it. I dated a girl my first three years in college. We did everything together. We lived together in a little apartment in Stockholm and had so much fun. When she decided a year ago to take a trip like this one, I couldn't go because of finances and school. She met a man while traveling and never came back. I still long for her and haven't dated much since." Janos' eyes left me and his gaze out over the lush countryside became very distant.

As we sat there physically in Nepal, we were both mentally half a world away in different countries. Love has a way of grabbing hold of you and not letting go very easily. Sometimes, I wonder whether it is worth the disruption it causes.

"Hey, look what the crazy Europeans put in my pack at lunch,"

Jon exclaimed, running up the hill while holding a large bottle of red wine and laughing. "You both look like you could use a little cheer. Come on; let's eat and be merry!"

I shot a couple of fast pictures to capture the sunset and my two friends being funny over a bottle of wine, and then I joined them. It had been a strange day. As I journaled before sleeping, I thought about parting with fellow trekkers I would never meet again, celebrating life in general with three men I knew nothing about, and missing a woman who I, in all likelihood, would never have the same relationship with again. Some days are just fuller than others.

SORCERER

We had decided the night before that we would get up early enough to be in Taplejung by around 8:00 a.m. We were up and on the trail by 5:00 a.m. It felt way too early, but as it turned out, it paid off. Before we had left Taplejung, we had talked to several locals who told us of a Tata truck that used a road none of us could find to deliver goods to Taplejung from a place near Cavalli. As we found out later, Tata is a brand name, and these trucks looked like the huge haulers that carry the rock in open pit mines. We hoped to catch the truck mid-day.

The trail was all downhill, so we made good time. I think we all were hungry, having not had breakfast. Late morning, we walked into the teahouse we'd stayed in two days earlier and ordered chapati and chai. While eating quietly and waiting for the Tata to arrive, I looked out the door of the cafe and saw a woman who had to be from the States.

"Good morning," I said. She couldn't see me at first in the dark restaurant.

"American?" she asked.

"Yes, Denver, Colorado, and you?"

"New York."

"You wouldn't be with the Peace Corps by any chance, would you?" I asked, my curiosity getting the better of me.

"Yeah, how did you know?"

"Your name would be Sharon Beimonier, I bet." I strung it out a little longer for the fun of it.

"Okay, come on; who are you?"

"All right," I said laughing. "My name is Keith, and I spent a night at a farm where I met a very eager young man who studies under you; he told me all about you."

"His name was Bhwani Prasad, I would venture to guess," she said with a knowing smile. While we talked, she entered the cafe and sat down. We shook hands, and I introduced her to my companions.

"We are trying to hitch a ride to Cavalli on one of those Tata trucks," I said, pointing to the parked vehicles outside.

"What's the problem?" Sharon asked.

"Well, the locals here have told us that we have to pay, but we don't know how much or to whom. The drivers were to have been here about now, so we're not sure that they're even going."

"Order me some chapati and chai, and I'll go see what I can do for you," she said while walking out of the teahouse.

The three of us sat eating and watched as she sent some young boys scurrying off down the street and she followed slowly. Out of a small building about a block away came the children with two

Nepali men. They all met in the middle of the road and had an animated discussion, talking fast and loud. Sharon turned around and walked back to us, and the men went back to the building from which they had emerged.

"They will take you for fifty rupees, and they will leave in half an hour," she said matter-of-factly as she sat down.

"That's great! Thank you; I guess it just takes a professional negotiator to get these things done," I replied.

"Oh, you just have to know how to talk to them. Most of the Nepalese are a good lot, albeit very lazy. Some of them, like these drivers, have ego problems and are stubborn."

As she talked to Jon and Janos, I sat and watched the three of them. She was twenty-six, with dark curly hair and big brown eyes. She wasn't very tall, probably 5' 2" and 120 pounds. With her New York accent, she seemed quite out of place, and yet her easy-going demeanor fit in well with her job. Soon, she would be leaving this region and going back to Kathmandu to teach. Obviously, she loved her work and being in Nepal. We quickly became friends, and then it was time to leave. She stood and watched as we got into the back of the dump truck, and then she waved to us until we were out of sight. I would have liked more time to visit with her and hear her story, but it wasn't meant to be. But as usual, just when I had needed some help, someone was there to assist me. My trip continued to be magical, and the more I observed it, the more evident that became.

For the first twenty minutes, the road was smooth and somewhat level; then it became steep and narrow with a severe drop-off on one side. All Nepalese roads seemed to be constructed this way, and you would think that I would have gotten used to them, but the driving skills of the Nepali left a lot to be desired. It was hard to squat and hold onto the side railing with the truck being tossed from side-to-side, and sitting down was too painful on your butt. I squeezed my pack between me and the railing to provide some cushion, and that seemed to help somewhat. Seeing me do this, my three companions did the same.

Back two, maybe three years before, I had seen a Roy Scheider movie titled *Sorcerer*. In it, Scheider was hired along with five other men to drive three truckloads of explosive nitroglycerin through the jungles of South America. They met with every imaginable obstacle, and the trucks that they drove looked just like these: huge, green, monolithic, ugly creations that were also extremely tough. They resembled a U.S. Army "Deuce and a Half" or 2.5-ton truck that you see in movies hauling soldiers or equipment, but even uglier, if that is possible. The truck that Scheider drove had the name "Sorcerer" painted on its side, and I nicknamed our truck the same.

As in the movie, we went across the wooden plank, suspension bridges that swayed and creaked badly. I was sure they wouldn't hold us, but they did. The drop was only five or six hundred feet. With my fear of heights, this was pushing my limits. However, it wasn't until we drove down a dry creek bed that it became awful. We only moved at one or two miles per hour, because the boulders we drove over were the size of Volkswagen Beetles. That lasted for more than an hour. Finally, the driver needed a rest. Hence, we stopped. He had to have been exhausted; I know we were.

We sat under a very tall, old tree and rested for ten minutes before moving on. After another hour, we arrived at the river near Cavalli. The road stopped because no bridge to cross on existed at the time. It was a short, ten-minute walk to the suspension footbridge that I'd crossed days earlier when I started my trek.

If I had known the road was there, I would have cut out much of my adventure; I'm glad I wasn't told how to get to it. The people I had met and stayed with were forever etched in my memory. By taking the more beaten path, we almost certainly encounter the mundane as well. It isn't always easy or popular to take the road less traveled, but either way, we must reap the rewards or consequences of our decisions. Looking back on most of the experiences in our lives, I think most people will take the road less traveled if they can get over the fear of the unknown. Predictability makes life boring, and this trip was anything but boring.

Basically, I hated Cavalli, although I rarely hate anything. This was the only Nepalese town I could say that about with ease. I knew that if we were to get the comfortable front seats on the next day's bus, I had better buy the tickets as soon as we arrived. While I did that, Zandra and the Swedes got our rooms at the same teahouse I had stayed at before. I had taken Janos aside and told him what the room should cost so that Zandra couldn't charge us more. As it turned out, he did try, but since Janos was prepared, he got the correct rate. Unfortunately, we were in two rooms right below the pigeons again.

The rest of the day was spent bathing, washing clothes, writing in journals, playing with local children, having a beer, and napping—an afternoon off, as it were. It felt extremely good. In this fashion, Cavalli wasn't too bad, I guess. By the time we ate dinner and went to bed, I felt calm and rested again.

Is This Bus Going to Make It?

We departed on the same beat-up bus that I had arrived on, with the same driver, the next morning at 6:00 a.m. Despite sitting in the front seats, conditions were a little cramped for Jon who was over six feet tall, but we were still better off than we would have been in the back. It had rained heavily overnight, and the result was a very slippery, muddy road.

Once again, the driver wasn't very kind to the bus as he drove along the rough road. The bus was full at Cavalli, and the weight of the passengers plus roof cargo made it bottom-out on some of the more severe bumps. We broke down three times in the first two hours because of broken leaf springs. Each time that happened, the routine was to unload the bus, jack it up, and pound pieces of old springs into the brackets. Then everyone would re-enter the bus until it happened again.

The ruts in the road, caused by heavy rains, were very deep, and the exposed rocks created by small rivers that crisscrossed the road from side to side made the ride very rough. In some places, the bus would drag bottom because the ruts and rivers were so deep, which also took away some of the driver's control in steering, especially around corners. Climbing up and out of the deep, lush valley surrounding Cavalli, we rounded a sharp corner too fast, dropped into a deep rut, veered out of control, and ran into the side of the mountain with a jolt. Everyone was thrown forward as the bus came to a violent halt. Babies and some women screamed and started to cry. People were strewn all about in the back of the bus, on the floor, and up over seats. I hit my head on the windshield and bounced back, feeling dazed.

The driver seemed confused and startled, but his mechanic was out of the bus and putting rocks under the back wheels like a veteran to keep the bus from rolling backward. After a couple of chaotic minutes, they instructed us once again to exit the bus and gather in front of it, while they inspected the damage. The steep, muddy road was hard to stand on, and many of the passengers fell as soon as they stepped off the bus. Janos' diarrhea had returned, so he was off into the trees. I wasn't sure whether this bout resulted from the scare of the accident, but it plagued him for the next two days.

It took the driver and his mechanic almost an hour of banging on the steering rods to bend them back into shape. This bus ride was becoming the ride from hell in a hurry, and I wanted it to be over. It was hard to believe such a beautiful day on the high roads of Nepal could be this uncomfortable. The forest's sounds and smells were pleasant enough that I just wanted to walk. But my still-healing blisters told me that wasn't a good idea. As I looked around at the passengers, I knew they had the same reservations and silently prayed for a safe journey. My feeling of *knowing* returned, and so did my confidence. I teased and played around with Jon and Janos. Soon many of the Nepali got caught up in the fun, and we all felt better. As the morning wore on, we only broke down two more times.

Uncertainty is something we all live with every moment of our lives. Most of us think that we have some control over life, only to discover in the end that we have had virtually none. I know that it is our ego that gives us the illusion of being in control. We don't want to accept that the uncertainty is what makes it all worthwhile. The excitement, fun, mystery, and thrill of life come from the not knowing. But being the intensely curious and controlling beings that we are makes the desire to understand and categorize everything almost obsessive.

It was on this trip that the essence of uncertainty appeared. The whole trip had been uncertain. Everything that I had planned had gone awry. But the *knowing* was as strong, if not stronger, than the uncertainty. I know that sounds crazy, but it's the only way I can describe it.

The very nature of being 10,000-plus miles from home causes you to detach from the fear of uncertainty about situations you have left behind. I found myself thinking of the woman I missed, but this perplexity became secondary as I faced the more immediate concerns of on-the-road survival. If I was ever going to see her again and deal with our problems, I had to get through the adventure at hand.

As we pulled into Phadim in a cloud of dust, I was very glad to de-bus and walk around for an hour, while our ever-dependable bus driver and his trusty sidekick banged our bus back into submission. Phadim was the epitome of the old saying, "You don't know how good you've got it until it's gone." This was a very poor little town. We found a small restaurant that served yum-yum noodles and beer, where we sat on a small, shaded veranda and talked about the morning's events.

The dust from the dirt streets coated everything, but the shop-keepers tried to stay ahead of it. They poured water on the street in front of their shops to stop the dust, but it only created mud that customers then carried inside. The experience felt like an old Western starring Clint Eastwood with a bandana over his face, as the ever-present wind whistled and blew dust everywhere.

We browsed the shops after lunch and bought a few trinkets to help the local economy. Then we walked back to our bus. Janos, still not feeling well, found a chair in the shade while Jon read his book, and I took some photos of the crew working on the bus. They all loved having their pictures taken. As soon as someone noticed what I was doing, they all stopped and posed in front of the bus. Greasy hands and clothing combined with big smiles and much laughter seemed to lighten the load of their day. I'm sure that their lives were very hard, but they took every opportunity to enjoy themselves.

In an hour or so, we were bouncing along the dirt road once again. We arrived in Illam at 8:00 p.m.—fourteen hours after we left Cavalli. There had been much to see, and I enjoyed it, but the ride was so rough that I ached all over from trying to hold on. I introduced my little band of travelers to the hotel I had stayed at on the trip to Cavalli; then we had dinner across the street. It took several servings of yum-yum and more than a couple of beers to soothe our weary bones and joints. I was very glad to get to bed, even if it was just my sleeping bag on a wooden cot.

GORBACHEV 1, CLINTON 0

During the night, I developed diarrhea, so I started taking the pills my doctor had given me before leaving the States. Consequently, I wasn't sleeping well—tossing and turning. All four of us were in the same room on separate cots, and the bathroom was downstairs on the second floor. I was feeling the effects of air pollution, exhaustion, poor food, and bad water. I felt a cough developing, and I had the symptoms of a cold coming on. I must have finally fallen asleep since I was suddenly awakened by my watch alarm going off. I had set it for an early wake-up so we could be sure to catch the bus and get our front seats again. The batteries in my flashlight failed after so much usage in two weeks, so I had to borrow Zandra's. I shut off my alarm and lay back for a moment until I was fully awake.

Jon's cot was behind mine; his feet near my head. I noticed that he was making some strange noises. Raising myself up on one elbow, I shined the flashlight on him and asked him whether he was all right.

"Jon! Jon, are you okay?" I shouted. He was thrashing back and forth in his sleeping bag; I could see that his eyes were staring straight out at nothing, and a small amount of foam was forming at the corners of his mouth.

"Janos, wake up! Jon is having a seizure!"

"He's what?" Janos replied in a state of confusion, having been awakened suddenly.

"I can't get my sleeping bag zipper to open. Roll him on his side so he won't swallow his tongue!" I hollered while frantically struggling with the stuck zipper.

Finally, I could get out of my sleeping bag and rushed to help Janos. Jon probably weighed 185 pounds, so he wasn't easy to move around, let alone confine to the cot. His seizure was strong and lasted close to two minutes. It was all that Janos and I could do to hold him down so he wouldn't hurt himself or swallow his tongue. At last, he started to relax and return to consciousness. He couldn't speak and was very dazed. I gave him a drink of water, and then with much difficulty, he told me he had pills to take for his epilepsy. Following his directions, I found them in his backpack, and he took one immediately.

We had to get ready for the bus. Janos and I hurriedly packed up our belongings and then started on Jon's. We told him to lie still and rest while we carried our packs to the bus, and then we would come back for him and his gear. Having never seen anyone have a seizure before, Zandra was quite amazed and more than a little leery of Jon. It was too much to try to explain to him; I didn't even try.

Before leaving the States, Pete and I had had lunch, and he had shared some interesting information. "I don't know how it will happen or when—it might not even be on this trip—but you will have an encounter where you will be placed in the position of needing the knowledge and a clear head to help someone through a medical emergency."

"Oh, really?" I replied.

"Yes. This event could be very serious, and you should be prepared for it."

Always the consummate psychic, Pete's words were full of his usual fare, but they had a ring of truth to them. You know what those times are like. Someone says something that is a little far-fetched, and still the small hairs on the back of your neck stand up, or you get that funny butterfly feeling in your stomach. At the time, I couldn't imagine what might possibly occur that I would have to aid in, but then I wasn't going to dismiss it totally either.

Jon wasn't in the best condition for most of the morning. He slept when I thought it was virtually impossible for anyone to sleep. The bus driver was back to his usual form, taking the curves too fast and bouncing through chuckholes. It felt like I was on an old stage-coach ride more than a bus ride. I was sure it would awaken Jon, but it didn't. By lunch, he was talking and returning to normal. He was very embarrassed by what had happened, and I tried to let him know that it was just part of his life that he needed to accept and not worry about. My first wife had epilepsy, and I shared with him the things she had gone through. This seemed to help him open up, talk about it, and we shared experiences for quite a while. He hadn't had a seizure in a long time, and he had thought he'd outgrown them. This episode had come as quite a surprise to him. From what I could remember, fatigue was a major player in the onset of seizures, as well as not taking the required medication regularly. I encouraged Jon to get a lot of rest in Kathmandu and not push himself for a while.

When we arrived in Badraphur, I had Zandra take a picture of the three of us before we went our separate ways. I had really wanted that picture to be a good one, but when I had the film processed at home, I found that Zandra had framed the shot, so our heads were missing. I was almost sure it was on purpose since I had put an end to his extortion of the Swedes and, ultimately, taken away the authority he had developed.

It was hard saying goodbye to Jon and Janos since we had been through a lot in a short time. I gave them both a hug after writing down their home addresses and phone numbers. They headed toward the bus to Kathmandu, and I to catch a bus to Bhaktupur. I was tired because of the way the day had started, and I was alone again for the first time in a few days: that gave my sense of adventure back to me. Bhaktupur at noon was bustling with buses arriving and departing; the air was filled with dust, diesel exhaust, smoke from open cooking fires, horns honking, and children playing and laughing—it all made for a chaotic atmosphere. Nevertheless, I was calm and happy. Happy to be somewhere different, living a life of curiosity and uncertainty, and loving every minute of it, I got on the bus headed to Karkarvita.

During the thirty-minute ride to Karkarvita, I sat next to two young Nepali men who were nineteen or twenty years old. One worked in a bank, and the other was a student. The banker was very friendly and gave me directions, while the student sat and observed me for a long time before speaking.

"I believe Bill Clinton is an awful President, and I hate his foreign policies. Gorbachev, on the other hand, is the savior of the common man," he said to me out of the blue.

"Well, we all are entitled to our opinion, aren't we?" I replied.

"Communism is the only way we can bring Nepal into the next century, and Gorbachev will help guide us," he continued, his defiant tone typical of a college student.

"I am so glad that you take such interest in your country's politics and future. It might be good for you to study the fall of communism in Eastern Europe in the last decade. Much has been learned about the differences between capitalism and communism that might benefit you also. Here is my stop, so I must go, but I have enjoyed talking with you."

"Harrumph," he snorted as I rose to leave the bus. The banker sat and smiled at me, nodding.

It took only a few minutes of walking to arrive at the border crossing and the customs compound. When the guard at the gate stopped me, I retrieved Suba's card from my pack and handed it to him.

"You are an American and are arriving from Illam?"

"Yes. I am to stay at Suba Shrestha's tonight," I replied.

"Please go to the customs office," he said, smiling and pointing at the building behind him.

I thanked him and proceeded to the building that housed the customs offices. Suba had left instructions for the employees to be on the lookout for me so they could take care of my needs, and it had started right off with this guard.

As I approached the building, Gopal saw me and came running with one of his underlings. They greeted me, smiling and saying a lot in Nepalese that I didn't understand, but they were happy to see me and to be of service. The helper took my pack and carried it to Suba's home, while Gopal took me into the adobe-style, one-story office building and made tea for me. He was proud to introduce me around to the men in the office. A ceiling fan whirred slowly as the men watched me drink my tea. They all sat behind old, wooden desks on very tattered, squeaky, green, army office chairs. Everything was covered with dust from the street. I'm sure they cleaned at the end of each day, but it was a hopeless exercise. They could tell that I was tired and didn't keep me long.

Gopal walked with me to Suba's house and let me in, asking whether I needed anything else. I told him that I needed a shower and to sleep for a while. My pack was already on the bed in the small guestroom I had occupied two weeks before. I quickly took off my clothes and went to the shower in the small building behind the home. The semi-warm water from the roof tank felt very good; I stood and enjoyed it for almost twenty minutes. Since Suba's family was gone to work for the day, I didn't feel too bad using it for so long.

When I'd finished cleaning up, I lay down and slept for three hours. I dreamt of the new girl I had met just before leaving the States. That seemed odd since I didn't know her very well, but it was a pleasant dream nonetheless. I awoke refreshed, and even my feet seemed to recover a little, being out of my boots for several hours. When I rose to walk, it was still difficult and painful, but better than a few days earlier.

I sat on the front porch for a while, writing in my journal and taking pictures of people, trucks, and dogs that wandered by. As I wrote I started to formulate a life philosophy that I would adopt when I returned home. New goals were getting clearer and my ultimate purpose was beginning to present itself. These realizations made me smile and excited at the prospect.

> AS I WROTE I STARTED TO FORMULATE A LIFE PHILOSOPHY THAT I WOULD ADOPT WHEN I RETURNED HOME. NEW GOALS WERE GETTING CLEARER AND MY ULTIMATE PURPOSE WAS BEGINNING TO PRESENT ITSELF. THESE REALIZATIONS MADE ME SMILE AND EXCITED AT THE PROSPECT.

Finally, feeling hungry, I thought I would go into Karkarvita to see whether I could find a small restaurant that served the yum-yum noodles I had come to know and love. But, as before, Gopal spotted me crossing the dirt compound and invited me in for chai. I had only been in the office for a few minutes when I was introduced to Rai, the chief customs officer. He sat and had chai and talked to all of us for almost an hour. I had dinner that evening at his home, which was pleasant since he had a cook and a houseboy who attended to our every need.

Rai spoke fair English and had visited the States in 1962. His hair was graying and was around fifty-five, although he looked much older. Once we got past the awkwardness of the language thing and not knowing each other, I genuinely enjoyed talking with him. Halfway through dinner, the city lost power and experienced a brownout; for the rest of the evening, we ate and talked by candlelight. The locusts were singing, and the air was warm and humid as I walked back to Suba's house. I was very tired from my trek and had no trouble falling asleep.

PART TWO

THANKSGIVING IN KATHMANDU

Rai had breakfast prepared for us before I left the next morning, and I then had my picture taken with him. He was a proud man, intelligent and wise. It would have been nice to spend a few more days with him, but my flight to Kathmandu was leaving in a couple of hours. Gopal drove me to the airport in Badraphur just before noon.

One of my regrets of the trip took place at the airport. I had a short time to wait, so I wrote in my journal and drank a cup of chai.

I watched a few other small commuter planes arrive and depart; each time, the siren in the tower would sound to warn anyone crossing the runway that a plane was approaching or taking off. There were no fences to keep people, cows, dogs, or anything else from meandering across the grass field. The simplicity of their systems was amazing, and yet they seemed to do quite well.

When it came time to board, I joined the other passengers in line and boarded a twelve-seater airplane. Just as all were seated and the door closed, I realized I was without the walking stick Pheriberi had given me. It was still leaning up against the terminal building where I had placed my pack earlier. I stood up quickly and tried to exit the plane, but the pilot asked me to be seated as he was starting to taxi. I tried to explain what I needed, but he wouldn't listen to my request and told me to be seated. We began to taxi as I locked my seatbelt in place.

I was dreadfully disappointed since the walking stick had been a gift from someone I never wanted to forget. It held a lot of memories from my trek, so its loss saddened me greatly. I could see it leaning up against the wall as we pulled away. In the years after my trek, in my mind, I would often see the walking stick in that place and long to have it. You may find it silly to feel an attachment to something like that, but it had such significance that I felt bad leaving it behind.

During the flight, as I watched Mt. Everest and the other majestic peaks of the Himalayas slowly pass by, I realized I was once again very calm and at peace. It was nice to be relaxed after the trials and tribulations of my trek. It had been a mystical time with many magical happenings—coincidences maybe—but I doubted it; things seemed to happen just when they were supposed to. Each time that I would totally detach and release the problem I was facing and a solution would appear. There seems to be a lot of power in detachment, yet we expend so much power avoiding it, not allowing it to happen. I will probably struggle with this concept for the rest of my life, but I hope I will continue to learn to let go and let life happen the way it's supposed to without being so caught up in the outcome of everything.

I was excited about getting back to Kathmandu and settling in at my favorite hotel, the Pothala. Most of all, it would be special to see my friends from the States, Bob and Denise, and our guide Tashi from my first trip with Denise. The next day was Thanksgiving, and spending it in Nepal would be different and fun. I was as happy at that moment as I had been in a long time.

In a few days, I would leave for my safari in Chitwan. For now, I had time to wander the streets of Kathmandu, doing some photography. Little did I know that some of the most exciting parts of my trip were still ahead of me. I thought most of the surprises were behind me, but that wasn't the case.

As much as I loved my trek to Taplejung, it was nice to return to Kathmandu. Each time I arrive in this city, it feels like a homecoming of sorts. Kathmandu is a city like many in this area of the world that have suffered too much growth too fast. Wars in Tibet and on the Pakistani/Indian border have sent a flood of refugees into both Nepal and India. Some of them may eventually return home, but many will establish themselves and stay.

As before, arriving at the Pothala Hotel made me feel at home. It's an older hotel that has a quaint charm to it. My room was small by American standards, but it had twin beds, a shower, a sink, and a flush toilet. These items would seem commonplace to most people, but after trekking without them, they were very welcome.

I wanted to do some shopping for friends and relatives. My feet were very glad to be in tennis shoes and on flat ground. I retrieved my additional gear and Denise's luggage from Lava's home, delivered it to the Pothala, and hit the streets. I found wandering Thamel, a suburb of Kathmandu, not at all like my first trip with Denise. The city had changed profoundly and not for the better in my eyes. On the other hand, it's hard to tell what is really better—the new Western ways of paved streets and satellite dishes or the old quaint shops and little restaurants. I suppose living conditions are better for the residents, but the pace is faster. It makes me wonder whether they will adhere to their religious and social convictions or become Westernized and materialistic.

During the morning, I spent time in Durbar Square with my camera and got some great shots of the old buildings and temples. At least that part of the city had retained its old-world feel. Cows still roamed the streets, and people sold fruit and vegetables at every intersection. It wasn't clean, but it was how these people had lived for centuries, and I would hate to see it go away. The sky was so blue, and through the haze, I could see the snow-capped Himalayas in the distance. The air was full of the odors of food cooking, meat spoiling in the sun, smoke from open fires, and the ever-present smell of urine. All the people were dressed in bright colors and sandals.

In just the three years between my trips, Kathmandu had become more congested. There were more cars and fewer bull-drawn carts.

The addition of satellite dishes everywhere and signs for Internet access really surprised me.

I know it sounds selfish, but I liked the city when it didn't have as many modern conveniences. I know the standard of living has risen, but at what price culturally? Many of the old buildings were being torn down in favor of new ones; in fact, new construction was everywhere, and it seemed as if there were more people from other countries than I had experienced before.

Over the years, I had been a devoted fan of *Star Trek*—the movies and various series. One of the edicts of the *Starship Enterprise*'s crew was always what they called the "Prime Directive." The focus of this directive was to keep a non-interference policy in the affairs of other cultures. It was a rule of compassion and respect, and I've always felt it should apply to our own world affairs. Sadly, getting the movers and shakers of this era to adopt that style of thinking would be near to impossible. Even though Nepal was being brought into the twentieth century as the rest of the world was leaving it,

I was not so sure the nation and its people were ready for it. They seemed to desire what the world had to offer, but the consequences would be many. This region of the world was the birthplace of so much spirituality. Buddhism and Hinduism have deep roots there, but the generations coming up now are faced with the draw of modern times, and they see the old as less exciting, I'm sure.

It was hard, as a tourist, not to have compassion and respect for the various cultures here, with their buildings, temples, and beliefs pre-dating Christianity by many centuries. As I wandered the old, narrow, cobblestone streets, I tried to imagine what it must have been like several hundred years ago or more. I thought of monks in their crimson robes; shopkeepers selling fruits, vegetables, and the exotic spices of the Orient; smoky restaurants on street corners, where meatless meals were prepared; the air filled with burning incense and fragrances of all kinds. And nowhere was there any indication of the outside world and the revolutions taking place: just a people taken care of by their benevolent king and loving gods. It was a time of slow lifestyles, meditation, and spirituality.

There were still hints of those old cultures everywhere. Many of the old buildings were so ancient that flowers, grass, and weeds grew from decaying tiled rooftops. The streets had been resurfaced with new cobblestones so many times that the doorways had become short enough that you had to bend way over to enter. Many of the wooden carvings still existed in the doorways, around windows, and on rooftops. Images of Buddha and Hindu gods were everywhere in brass and wood.

Several months earlier, I had planned to meet Bob and Denise while they were on a yearlong trip around the world. We timed my stay in Kathmandu with their arrival so we could spend Thanksgiving together. We would only have a few days, but it would be fun to meet, rest, and get caught up on each other's lives. Then I would head for Chitwan in the south, and they would trek to Mt. Everest before traveling on to India.

It was fun to take my time and wander the city, snapping photos and shopping. The city, with its hustle and bustle, was different from the mountains, yet it was faintly similar. Nearly everyone I made eye contact with smiled at me; some would offer a "Namaste" in passing while others would just nod. Occasionally, I stopped for a chai or beer and rest in the sun, grateful for the ability to be moving so leisurely. To enjoy a city fully, you must move slowly and take your time. There are always little nooks and crannies that hold mystery until explored, and with them come the sense of adventure and the possibility of discovering something you might never have seen if you hadn't followed your curiosity. Some of my best purchases came from small, out-of-the-way shops that carried statues of Buddha or a Hindu god or old coins that you couldn't find anywhere else.

Many of my treasured photos came from places where I would find a child, small temple, or flower pot in my path lit perfectly by the sun. These places exemplified the old proverb, "A picture is worth a thousand words." Photography is an art form I have come to love and appreciate. Only in painting can you come as close to the real existence and essence of people and places. I can get lost for hours taking photos, then my love of writing takes over, and I get to express myself in words complemented by the shots—what a wonderful combination.

It had taken me many years to come to the realization that I was not following my heart. My passions existed in the creation of art through photos and writing, and once I discovered that my spirituality occupied the same space, the decision to live a more creative life came easily. Sometimes I feel as though I wasted a lot of time getting here, but then I realize that it all happened just as it was supposed to. I couldn't enjoy what I enjoy today without those experiences to guide and prod me along.

Discovering your passions goes a long way to developing your life philosophy and purpose. If you can find them, you often discover your purpose hidden in them. As my speaking was coming into view, my writing and photography were being refined and I was writing my life philosophy as I progressed. There are some core values and virtues that stay the same but we have to re-evaluate our philosophy as we move along life's path. It's a constant change because of how we evolve as individuals with new life experiences. I knew I would write and re-write mine numerous times in the years to come and that's wonderful because hopefully it would show growth.

After shooting four rolls of film and several hours wandering, I made it back to my hotel in the late afternoon and took a nap. I awakened feeling hungry, went in search of something different, and settled on Greek food. On my first trip, Denise and I had eaten at a small, second story Greek restaurant, I remembered it as being close to authentic, about 20-minutes later, I found it. After eating dinner, I was still tired; I journaled quickly, went right to bed, and slept like a baby. It was comforting to be in a place where I felt confident of my surroundings and could let go and relax deeply.

Drifting off to sleep, I could hear the small sounds from the street below of a city getting ready for the night. I smelled the cinnamon rolls from Narayan's restaurant beneath my room and knew what I'd be having for breakfast.

> THERE ARE SOME CORE VALUES AND VIRTUES THAT STAY THE SAME BUT WE HAVE TO RE-EVALUATE OUR PHILOSOPHY AS WE MOVE ALONG LIFE'S PATH. IT'S A CONSTANT CHANGE BECAUSE OF HOW WE EVOLVE AS INDIVIDUALS WITH NEW LIFE EXPERIENCES.

GOODBYE, B.J.

During my trip to Nepal in '92, Denise and I both fell in love with the country. We were good friends, like brother and sister almost, and it proved to be an interesting experience to travel with a woman with whom I wasn't involved. She and Bob married a year after we returned, and we remained good friends until life took us off in different directions and we lost touch.

Their flight was to arrive at 1:00 p.m. I got to the airport at 12:30 p.m. and immediately ran into Tashi Lama. We had become friends; so much so that Denise frequently faxed letters to him. I had no idea that he was going to meet their plane also; he recognized me right away, and we laughed at the coincidence.

Shortly after that, we learned that Denise's plane was going to be three hours late. We decided to eat lunch and get caught up on what had been going on in our lives for the previous three years.

Tashi shared with me that he returned to his home and family near Everest each spring for a visit. The rest of each year had been spent guiding people like me around Nepal in the Himalayas. He had aged somewhat, but he still had the bright eyes, smile, and personality that Denise and I had come to love during the two weeks we spent with him in 1992. Tashi was thirty years old and 5' 3"; he was small by Western standards, but his heart and loving energy made him seem much larger.

Tashi was a Sherpa and his last name, Lama, meant that he was in line to live with the Dalai Lama. The Sherpas live in the region near Everest and make excellent guides because of their conditioning living at high altitudes. They also are very well-known for saving the people they guide. Folklore abounds with stories of their feats carrying climbers or trekkers for days in the mountains to return them to safety after an accident or illness.

During our trek to Annapurna, I had sprained my right ankle, and Tashi had offered to carry me, but the injury wasn't that bad, and with the aid of a walking stick, I did okay. He took my pack and carried it along with his own, staying by my side until he knew I was okay. The depth of the Sherpas' compassion was amazing to witness firsthand, and it made me a true believer in all the folklore.

Over the years that he had been a guide and porter, Tashi had scaled many peaks in the Himalayas. He was also in demand because he was an excellent cook. He proudly wore a baseball cap from an expedition in '92 he had been on where he had performed as the cook for the climbers. His dark skin always contrasted with the whiteness of his teeth, and his smile was the first thing you noticed about him. Right away, he gave you a sense of confidence and friendship, and I could understand why he was always in demand by new trekkers, as well as old friends like Denise and Bob.

When Bob and Denise finally cleared customs, we returned to the Pothala and got settled in. By then, we were all hungry, so we went out for dinner. It wasn't until halfway through dinner that I realized how much I was enjoying this rendezvous. As I sat and watched three good friends laugh and talk, it came to me how much friendship adds to our lives. I do truly believe that our souls have known each other before coming to earth: that during many lifetimes together, we have become so connected that we feel a deep sense of comfort with certain people.

Friends come and go during our lifetimes, and when someone returns and you pick up right where you left off, you know it is one of those soul relationships. If you take this concept a step further, you also realize that it gives you a sense of confidence in the longevity of our existence—that we do have eternal life and that we will have our friends and family in the next life, too. Now, whether we will be in the same form as we are here in the earthly plane has yet to be discovered, but the fact that we are all learning together in this experience leads us to believe that we will leave this plane and be reunited in the next.

Friendship is a unique concept. We find it in the most unlikely places—offered by people we want it from and by others we don't. I first met Denise in the Customer Service Department at my bank. I had an office in the same building, so it made it easy for me to correct the errors in my ever-out-of-balance checkbook.

I've always liked women much more than men, and I've always found it easy to make friends with them. Denise wore the most unusual earrings, and as I teased her about them, over time, we became friends. During the fall of 1991, Denise and her boyfriend Bob stopped seeing each other for a while, but they remained very close, and they ultimately married in 1993. My divorce, in 1990, was still fresh, and new romantic endeavors were lukewarm. On New Year's Eve 1991, Denise and I shared too much wine and pizza. She told me she was planning to take a trip and showed me an atlas map of

Asia and Nepal. The idea of a trip like that sounded good to me, so I offered to go along. I'm sure she wanted to go alone, but over the next few months, the trip began to take shape. We left in late September and were gone for almost a month.

A trek was planned through our Nepalese travel agent, Sam Shrestha in Denver, and he arranged for Tashi Lama to be our guide. Tashi showed up at our room in Kathmandu the night before our trek was to begin. We were to fly to Pokhara; Tashi and our porter, Ganu, would go by bus overnight and meet us there the next day. Tashi seemed small and shy, but we both felt he was a nice young man. Over the next four days, we trekked on a popular route from Pokhara to Dhampus, New Bridge, and Chomrong, ultimately arriving at the Machapuchare Base Camp.

Along the way, we had contracted the Kathmandu crud (flu) and felt awful, with a fever and coughing. That strain of flu isn't pleasant, even if you're home in bed. We met some trekkers who were on their way out of the region, and they gave us their supply of antibiotics. It took a couple of days for them to work, but they definitely helped. Luckily, Ganu was carrying the bulk of our gear, and we did stay in teahouses each night, so things could have been much worse.

We were trekking up and down steep hills. The rocky trail switched back and forth, then over streams and through bamboo forests. The valleys were deep and lush, and you could see a long way when you were on top of a ridge. When you were in the bottom of a valley, the vegetation was thick, beautiful, and smelled clean and fresh. It was almost like you were walking through an oxygen machine.

The teahouses we stayed at were small, tin- or thatched-roofed, single or two-story, brick or rock structures. They had no electricity or running water but did have padded benches used as bunks, upon which we threw our sleeping bags. We received dhal baht dinners and chapati, jam, and chai breakfasts. Sometimes they had porridge, which was wonderful.

Each morning was cold, the temperature dipping to the low forties then the afternoons it warmed up; we took off layers of clothes as the day progressed, only to turn around and put them back on in the late afternoon. During the day, Tashi took great care of us and saw to our every need. He knew we were sick so he would let us stop to rest often, and whenever possible, he would bring milk, tea or mandarin oranges to us if the children in the small villages were selling them.

The trip with Denise had an important side story. Before leaving Denver in '92, I received a phone call from a close friend named Mary.

"Hi, Keith. It's Mary."

Even over the phone, I could tell she was crying softly. Mary was a good friend and an agent with the same company I worked for. She lived forty miles away in Boulder, and we got together for lunch frequently. We had become friends, sharing the usual stories around the office about clients and their problems If it hadn't been for Mary, I wouldn't have pursued the metaphysical relationship that followed. She kept hounding me to meet with her and Pete to have a spiritual discussion. Being one of my best friends, she knew almost everything about me and me about her. Mary was one of those friends who is the glue that holds life together when you are coming apart at the seams.

"Mary, what's wrong?"

"You know my friend, B.J., who lives in Aspen, the one who has been to Nepal many times? Well, he died a couple of days ago."

"Oh, Mary, I'm so sorry; are you okay?"

"Well, I went to the funeral, and afterward, some of us had to attend a reading of his will. At that meeting, I found out that he wanted his ashes to be strewn in the Rockies and in the Himalayas. I have a favor to ask of you. Since you are leaving for Nepal in a few days, would you take a small vial of his ashes and spread them at the highest point you travel to?"

At this point, she started to cry again. I felt so badly for her. B.J., who had been in his late seventies, had been a mountaineer and trekker for many years. Obviously, the tie between him and Mary was close. I couldn't refuse even if I wanted to.

"I'd be honored to spread them for you. When can we get together?"

"Well, I can meet you tomorrow if you like. However, there is one more part you must do. One of B.J.'s hiking buddies has written a poem, and we would like it very much if you would read it and get pictures of where you do the service."

"That's no problem. I'll be glad to help out in any way I can."

It is common for trekkers and hikers worldwide to have instant camaraderie. You bond easily, having nature and the mountains in common. This request only made my trip more special. I felt an additional purpose; one that had a unique significance. Little did I know it would affect me for a long time to come.

On the third night of that trip, we stayed in the beautiful hillside town of Chomrong. It faces northeast and is covered with rice paddies terraces and a few trees. In the distance, you can see the tip of Machapuchare and most of Dhaulagiri, two in the highest peaks of the region and, certainly, two of the prettiest. Snow-covered and majestic, they constantly glow against the blue sky. Our teahouse had a grassy lawn with picnic tables for the trekkers and a small staff that would serve beer, water, and small snacks. We had met a group from England, Amsterdam, and Australia and spent the afternoon talking and enjoying the sun and rest.

During the night, Denise got sick to her stomach. Because our bunk beds were next to each other, she woke me up and asked me to help her get outside. With only the light from our flashlights, we made our way down the aisle between the bunks of other trekkers, then down a ladder, through the kitchen, and out to the grassy area in front of the building.

It was 2:30 a.m. and the full moon lit up the snowcapped peaks so brightly that you could read a newspaper. The air was crisp and not a sound could be heard, except Denise losing her dinner.

I felt sorry for her. Still, I couldn't help laughing, because, between vomiting, she said, "If I have to be sick or die (vomit) ... what a beautiful place to do it (vomit) ... It's so beautiful!" She was on her hands and knees, sick as a dog, and she still found her sense of humor. Luckily, she felt much better the next morning.

We continued to rise in altitude over the next two days and then broke out above the timberline. We passed the remnants of winter, frozen waterfalls, and huge drifts of snow that probably never totally melted. The green landscape of the valleys behind us gave way to the brown rock and tundra of the high country.

We were exhausted when we reached the Machapuchare Base Camp on the fifth day. After some discussion with Tashi, we decided to stay there an extra day to rest and acclimate to the 14,000-plus foot altitude. By then, we hadn't had a bath for several days; we had Tashi ask the cook to boil a pot of water so Denise could wash her hair, and then both of us could get a sponge bath of sorts. We took turns in my room cleaning up, and it felt great. The temperature was only in the twenties, and the warm water really helped. Our rooms weren't heated; to keep my things from freezing during the night, I slept with them in my sleeping bag: film, contact lens solution, and some water. Denise ended up in a different room with a doctor and his daughter from England. I stayed with an Aussie the first night.

As the Aussie and I were preparing to go to sleep, he asked me whether I was the fellow the guides and porters had talked about up and down the trail who snored badly. Unfortunately for him, I was. Even Denise and Tashi had teased me about it, but I had no idea that word had spread that much; it was embarrassing. He kept kicking my bunk during the night to wake me and temporarily stop my incessant snoring. I felt so sorry for him, but I couldn't help it.

He arose and left at 3:45 a.m. to make the ascent to the

Annapurna Base Camp for sunrise. Denise, Tashi, and I left at 7:45 a.m. It only took a couple of hours, but it was worth the climb because the view was spectacular. The Annapurna Base Camp is surrounded by a horseshoe of 26,000-plus-foot peaks: Annapurna I & II, Dhaulagiri, Hinchuli, Gang Puma. At the open end, Machapuchare stands alone, snow-covered and majestic, as the only unclimbed mountain in Nepal. The Nepalese government wants to retain it as a national monument and has never issued any climbing permits for it.

The sky is said to be almost black at the summit of Mt. Everest, but here it was a very dark blue. The air was very cold, and the only wildlife we saw were huge copper-colored birds, circling above us, riding the high mountain currents. Small, colorful wildflowers bloomed where there was enough sun all day; otherwise, the only colors were the green and brown tundra and the brown and steel blue rock of the landscape. High above us, we could hear the periodic roar of an avalanche as snow gave way to gravity. Occasionally, we could see one racing down a mountainside; luckily, they were too high to reach us.

When we arrived at the Annapurna Base Camp, it was time to hold B.J.'s service. We made our way to a high point above the camp where we had a clear view of the valley below and the Himalayas above.

Denise said she would take my camera and record the service. I removed my pack and retrieved the small glass vial, the envelope containing the poem, and my camera. While I was doing that, nine more trekkers reached our location. They were people we had passed on the trail over the past two days, and they wondered whether they were too late for the service. I was amazed and touched by their desire to be included. Our international gathering expanded, even more, when we were joined by two trekkers from England, one from Amsterdam, three from New Zealand, and three Germans.

"As many of you know, just before leaving the U.S., I was

contacted by a close friend with the news of the death of a friend of hers. His name was B.J., and he had been to Nepal many times, once to help nurse my friend during a serious illness. In his will, B.J. asked to have his ashes spread over the Himalayas and the Rocky Mountains of Colorado where he had lived until his death. I was honored when asked to do this service, and I am also pleased that so many of you have chosen to be here as well.

"I didn't know B.J., and yet I did; we all did. B.J. was just like so many of us, having a spirit for the adventurous side of life, the side that yearns for the connectedness with nature that only trekking in the mountains can give you. The spirit to travel in faraway lands and unusual cultures that need to be seen and appreciated for what they are today. Nepal represents the epitome of that drive—beautiful, serene, spiritual, mysterious, and yet so familiar. When I arrived in Kathmandu during my first trip to Nepal, I had a sense of returning home, and it brought tears to my eyes. I'm sure that many of you who have visited here before shared in that kind of homecoming.

"My friend Mary has sent along with the ashes a poem that a friend of B.J.'s wrote that I'm to read now."

I came here with the wind, so very long ago,
Or perhaps not so long at all, as history is wont to show.
And spent some time with you,
Watched fortunes ebb and flow,
Through wars and struggles, hopes and dreams,
In life, that's ours to know.
Do not hold me here, I pray,
For my soul has need to grow.
But if you ask me, I will stay,
Such is love that binds us so.
My soul is now unbound, you see,
To learn and travel endlessly.
There's a universe in store,

And it's my nature to explore.
If you would seek me, go outside in nature,
Find my essence there,
Where we can secret dreams confide,
Among bird's song that fills the air.
I'll walk with you 'round rocks and trees,
And celebrate life's harmonies,
Or sit with you in noonday sun,
No obligation—just for fun.
We'll traverse water, ice, snow,
The peaks above, valleys below,
To see the beauty, symmetry,
And learn about integrity.
Much truth abounds in nature fair,
But my essence is the air.
So raise your eyes up to the sky,
For, as you know, I love to fly.
And I will come. Sit quietly,
On a grassy knoll and wait for me.
And know when gentle breezes blow,
That I come with the wind, and with the wind I go.

When I looked up from the piece of paper in my hand, I saw, through eyes filled with tears, the emotion that had touched everyone there. Many were wiping their eyes; some were sitting with arms around each other, while others simply stared at the ground in solitude. I took out the vial and held it high, and I slowly poured out the contents into a gentle breeze that carried B.J.'s ashes out into the Nepal sky. Quietly and to myself, I said, "Goodbye, B.J."

The trek back to the Machapuchare Base Camp was a somber one. The three of us took our time and didn't talk much. The altitude made us slow in our movements, and we tired easily, so by the time we returned to Base Camp, we were ready to warm up and rest.

The friendship that I forged with Denise during those days is one I'll always treasure. We worked through the physical pains of trekking and the growing pains of two people getting to know each other under unusual conditions. During the last days of the trip, we understandably got on each other's nerves, but the friendship was cemented.

They say we make only a small number of true friendships in our lives, and I've been lucky to find and enjoy mine. We must emit an energy to attract the people who become meaningful in our lives. It is truly a wonderful gift to have these relationships to rely on in bad times and to revel in during good times.

"Keith. Earth to Keith, where are you?" Denise asked teasingly.

Startled, I suddenly realized that I had been deep in my memories of our first trip. As we ate and laughed, we also became tired. It had been a full day. It was the time for our sleepy little band of friends to return to the Pothala for a good night's sleep. I journaled and fell asleep, feeling warm, comfortable, and in God's hands. That is an experience everyone should have.

> THEY SAY WE MAKE ONLY A SMALL NUMBER OF TRUE FRIENDSHIPS IN OUR LIVES, AND I'VE BEEN LUCKY TO FIND AND ENJOY MINE. WE MUST EMIT AN ENERGY TO ATTRACT THE PEOPLE WHO BECOME MEANINGFUL IN OUR LIVES. IT IS TRULY A WONDERFUL GIFT TO HAVE THESE RELATIONSHIPS TO RELY ON IN BAD TIMES AND TO REVEL IN DURING GOOD TIMES.

PASTIPATINATH

I'd become so accustomed to being alone and writing that I arose early on purpose to come down to Narayan's Restaurant on the main floor of the hotel to write. I was sure it would be a while before the others got up. We had spent the balance of the prior day getting Bob and Denise settled-in, retrieving their mail at the American Express office, exchanging luggage, etc. I gave them several pieces of luggage that I had brought on my flight, full of things they had packed before leaving some months ago. Since Nepal would be the coldest portion of their trip, they had known they would need different clothing here. They would sell or give it all away when they left for India.

We had talked, extensively, the night before because they had experienced a lot on their trip so far and I had a lot of news from home to bring them. To that date, they had been to China, Vietnam, and Thailand. I was a little envious, as I'm sure most people would be, at the wonderful opportunity Bob and Denise had to tour the world at the ripe old age of thirty-something. By the same token, I was happy for them.

The day before had gone by quickly with shopping and sightseeing and doing the odds-and-ends errands we all needed to do before we went our separate directions. On our way back to the hotel in the evening, I ran into Jon and Janos. It was wonderful to see them and to know that Jon was all right after the seizure he had experienced on our last day together. I had been wondering about them and was glad for the opportunity to put my mind at ease. They were going to India in a few days and seemed to be having a good time. I was tired when I finally went to bed, and I slept very soundly.

That morning, Kathmandu was shrouded in a thick blanket of the wonderfully, moist, fog. Earlier, when I had arrived at Narayan's, I had made a point of sitting at a window table so I could watch the people of Thamel scurry along in the mist. If I have a favorite thing in life that I don't get to experience very often, it's fog. I find fog comforting. It's generally cool, so people are dressed a little more warmly and are moving a little faster to their destinations. Since you can't see very far, your world condenses.

With that closeness, I sense the immediate area around me with greater awareness. Sounds come to you differently: more muffled and non-directional. The air smells of the dampness, more like nature in the raw. I just love it.

Looking out my window through the fog, I could see the shop of an Oriental rug dealer, a photo processing shop, an alley, and a bookstore. Motor scooters puttered by with as many as four people on them—Mom, Dad, and two kids. I'd like to see them try that in the States, although it was a very common sight over here.

Here in Narayan's, I was comfortable and warm; I had ordered chai and toast with mandarin jam—what a great way to start your day. Crackly sitar music was playing over an old speaker in the corner, and the place smelled of cinnamon and tea. There was one Chinese couple, one German couple with a baby, two young Frenchmen, and me—an international and eclectic bunch we were.

The lighting was low, but I had enough light from the street to write. It was a nice, little restaurant. I wasn't sure when it was built, but it looked late '70s vintage. There were wooden tables and chairs, cream-colored walls with brown trim, and dark brown linoleum floors. Around the cash register, bakery goods were for sale. The glass in the display case was cracked on one end and covered with duct tape.

———————

THE OLD PHRASE, "BE CAREFUL WHAT YOU WISH FOR BECAUSE YOU MIGHT JUST GET IT," POPPED INTO MY HEAD AS I WROTE ABOUT LIVING THERE. WE DON'T REALIZE THE POWER WE HUMANS HAVE TO MAKE OUR WISHES COME TRUE. IF YOU HAVE A REAL INTENT TO DO SOMETHING, AND YOU IMAGINE WHAT IT WOULD BE LIKE, HARD ENOUGH AND LONG ENOUGH, MOST OF THE TIME IT WILL COME TO PASS. THE MORE YOU RECOGNIZE THIS POWER AND EXERCISE IT, THE EASIER IT IS TO MANIFEST YOUR DREAMS. HUMANS HAVE POWERS TO DO ALL SORTS OF THINGS AND ARE JUST SCRATCHING THE SURFACE OF THOSE ABILITIES. LIKE WHEN WE DREAM OF SOMETHING WE REALLY WANT FOR A LONG TIME

AND THEN IT BECOMES A REALITY, OR WHEN
SOMEONE PRAYING FOR A PATIENT HEARS THE
PATIENT HAS MIRACULOUSLY HEALED FROM
A SERIOUS ILLNESS. THESE ARE POWERS WE
POSSESS, BUT BECAUSE WE LOOK AT THEM AS
FLUKES RATHER THAN INHERENT ABILITIES, WE
NEVER GROW THEM.

WE HAVE ALL SORTS OF HIDDEN ABILITIES
THAT WE NEVER DISCOVER BECAUSE WE DON'T
TAKE THE TIME TO GET TO KNOW AND LOVE
OURSELVES. I USED TO TELL AN ALCOHOLIC
FRIEND OF MINE THAT AS SOON AS SHE LEARNED
TO LOVE HERSELF, SHE WOULDN'T MISTREAT
HERSELF THAT WAY ANYMORE. SHE COULD
NEVER GET A GRIP ON THE CONCEPT OF SELF-
LOVE AND LET HER INNER-SELF GUIDE HER.

WE ARE ALWAYS LOOKING OUTSIDE OF
OURSELVES FOR GRATIFICATION IN ONE WAY
OR ANOTHER WHEN TRUE HAPPINESS EXISTS
IN DISCOVERING OUR TRUE POTENTIAL AND
PURSUING IT. TAKE MY WRITING FOR INSTANCE;
I NEVER READ MUCH AND DIDN'T LIKE TO
WRITE. WHILE WORKING WITH A THERAPIST
AFTER A DIVORCE, I WAS TOLD TO JOURNAL
EACH EVENING TO HELP GET MY FEELINGS OUT.

WHEN I SAT DOWN TO WRITE THE FIRST NIGHT, THE POETRY THAT CAME OUT OF THE END OF MY PEN SURPRISED ME GREATLY. FIVE YEARS LATER, I HAD TAKEN MY POETRY AND LOVE OF PHOTOGRAPHY AND PUBLISHED MY FIRST BOOK. TALENTS SURFACE WHEN YOU LEAST EXPECT THEM, AND THEY ARE OFTEN THE ONES YOU SHOULD FOLLOW.

THERE IS SO MUCH POWER IN CHOOSING TO FOLLOW YOUR TALENTS AND SEEING WHERE THEY TAKE YOU. WHEN YOU DO, THE UNIVERSE OPENS DOORS THAT IT WOULDN'T BEFORE. THERE IS POWER IN TAKING ACTION. IF YOU JUST SIT ON THE COUCH AND SAY, "GEE, I WISH I WERE GOOD AT ACTING," NOTHING WILL EVER HAPPEN. BUT IF YOU TAKE THE FIRST STEP BY ENROLLING IN ACTING CLASSES, SUDDENLY, OPPORTUNITIES WILL OPEN UP THAT YOU NEVER THOUGHT POSSIBLE. INTENTION WITHOUT ACTION IS LIKE FISHING WITHOUT A HOOK.

Several men were baking in the kitchen, while others waited tables. There were no women employees at all. The back entrance connected to a small patio and garden area off the hotel lobby. On warmer days, I liked to sit out there in the sun, but today, the foggy street view was more attractive, peaceful, and calm. I could have lived there—writing, meditating and just being.

Denise joined me at the table; we shared breakfast and then went shopping. It was fun to be with just her for a while.

At noon, we returned to the hotel to pick up Bob and go to Pastipatinath. It's a beautiful religious retreat that is home to many old monasteries, temples, and cremation altars. The Baghmati River, considered sacred, flows through the middle of the compound. Any river that ultimately flows into the Ganges is considered holy. The funeral pyres and cremation platforms sit along the side so the ashes can be pushed into the water. It's quite a sight to watch a body wrapped in ceremonial white cloth burn on top of a large stack of logs. The flames reach ten feet in the air when the fire is at its peak.

Many different activities take place in the river at the same time, as life continues for the living. Upstream fifty yards from the cremation, two women were filling large brass pots with water for the day; below them at forty yards, a man was washing his clothes and then giving himself a bath in the noonday sun. Below the cremation, ten yards or so, a couple of young boys held nets in the water in hopes of finding the jewelry of the deceased in the floating ashes. Of course, the water is a murky brown, and at this time of year, it only spans thirty yards and maybe eighteen inches deep. During the rainy season, it swells to one hundred feet across and several feet deep.

Pastipatinath is a favorite place of mine for meditation and photography. The combination of centuries-old temples, stupas, and monasteries, along with monks and monkeys, makes for an ideal place for both. I'm always in awe of the ancient and sacred beauty of this place. It covers many dozens of acres and is the home to both Hindu and Buddhist temples. The main Hindu temple is guarded, and you must be a Hindu to enter, but what little I could see through the entrance looked beautiful, with many colors, plus polished brass gods everywhere. It almost made me want to join just so I could gain entrance.

Certain mystical places in the world are said to have wonderful energy like Sedona in Arizona, Jerusalem, and the Mayan ruins of

Belize. Pastipatinath is one of them also. When I sat quietly near the temples and meditated, the depth of the meditation and sense of peace were more powerful than I had experienced anywhere else. It was as if I had entered a place where I was so close to God and God's universe that my entire being was encompassed in that spiritual energy. The ease of meditation and the calmness was breathtaking; I felt truly connected. I'm sure people come here who are not affected by the energy, but if they let themselves be aware of their own energy, they too will find a peace that is quite remarkable.

The ever-present sacred cows wandered the area, and children begged to be your guide or just for money. The smell of jasmine incense floated through the air, making me feel like I had just stepped back several hundred years in time.

An old monk called the "Milkman" allowed people to take his picture for money or a gift. He lived only on milk and products that could be mixed with milk, like chocolate. He had never cut his hair, which was braided and wound around his head many times. His tan and weathered face, curious eyes, and bright smile made him a wonderful photographic subject, and he seemed to enjoy the attention. He sat in his crimson and gold robes near a bridge that crossed the Baghmati and watched life come and go. I wished I knew more of the language and could talk to him; he would, I was sure, have many fascinating tales to relate.

Earlier in the day, I had calculated what time it would be at home and called my parents to wish them a Happy Thanksgiving and let them know I was okay and thinking of them. They were surprised and pleased to hear from me, and I was glad they were healthy and doing fine.

In the evening, Bob, Denise, and I went to a fancy Indian place for Thanksgiving dinner and then made an early night of it. I would leave for Chitwan early the next morning, and they would rendezvous with Tashi to take a helicopter to Namche Bazar near Mt. Everest. After journaling and slowly falling asleep, I regretted that we had only had a short time together, but at the same time, I was very grateful for the time we'd had. I also knew it was time for me to get on with my time alone, for I still had many things to discover. I wondered what new revelations would present themselves and what I would learn from them. When you look forward to each day with excitement, life glows.

CHITWAN

The trip to Chitwan was uneventful and relaxing. Shyam Shrestha had arranged for a car with a driver to take me to the safari camp. It still took several hours, but the roads going south were much better than those near Kanchenjunga in the northeast. We followed the Pokhara River much of the way, and the farther we went, the larger it became.

I had become so relaxed in Kathmandu that I fell asleep in the car for a while. My driver had brought a friend along to keep him company, and they spoke softly to each other and left me alone. I preferred that to someone who was into talking. It was nice to sit in the backseat of the little Toyota and watch the Nepali countryside roll by. It changed a great deal from the foothills of the Himalayas to the low lands. The flat land was green and lush.

My driver stopped and asked for directions, saying that we were close to my destination. When they left me by the side of the road, I wondered where I was and whom I was to meet. This was the first time during my trip that I felt disappointed with myself. During my trek, I was to blame for getting lost, but that, to some extent, was fun. Here, I had left my welfare up to someone else, who had brought me to a place where I had no idea what to do next.

Luckily, in a few moments, a Land Rover pulled up with a safari camp logo on its side, and a very friendly chap gathered up four of us, who were all standing together, and shuttled us off to his camp. Unfortunately, that was not where I was supposed to be. My driver had left me about five miles from my camp and at the wrong stop. It took only a few minutes to figure this out when my name wasn't on the check-in sheet for new guests. The friendly camp manager started calling other camps to find out where I was to be delivered. He made me very comfortable, with a cold drink and a place to sit in the shade, while he sought an answer to the mystery of where I was to be. Only forty minutes later, I was given a ride to my camp, and a new guide, named Godi, greeted me with apologies and a beer. We were instant friends and really enjoyed each other over the next few days.

Godi was a pleasant young man with a soft voice and a gentle confidence, which I liked right off. He had lived near Chitwan for a long time and was married with two children. Chitwan is a large game reserve on both the India and Nepal sides of the border. So many animals were lost to hunting by both peoples that the two governments formed the reserve to give refuge to the area's animals.

Godi took me to see the elephants and for a walk by the river before sunset. Speaking of sunsets, I have seen some that were spectacular in my life, but these had to rank right up there with those in Vietnam. Wonderful colors that a camera just can't capture, but

I tried anyway. He showed me many birds and how the elephants were cared for at the end of a day's work.

Back at the camp, I met the manager, Phalad. He informed me that he was out of beer and invited me to walk along with him to the village a short way down the trail. Along the way, he shared his "love life troubles" with me in a rare display of male bravado. He was dating two women, one twenty-nine and the other fifteen; he was twenty-two. They each wanted him, and he wanted both and couldn't make up his mind; then there was furthering his education and running the camp. Oh well, so many decisions. At twenty-two, life is the same the world over.

———

BEFORE DINNER, AS I SAT WATCHING THE BRILLIANT ORANGE AND RED SUNSET IN MY NEW PARADISE, I TOOK THE TIME TO THINK MORE ABOUT THE POWERS WE HUMANS ENJOY. WE HAVE SO MANY THAT WE TAKE FOR GRANTED, LIKE THE POWER OF CHOICE. EACH DAY, WE MAKE MAJOR DECISIONS REGARDING OUR LIVES AND MINOR ONES LIKE WHAT DRESSING TO HAVE ON OUR SALAD AT LUNCH.

I HAD MADE A CONSCIOUS DECISION TO COME TO NEPAL ALONE. THAT ONE CHOICE HAD GIVEN ME TIME ALONE TO DISCOVER NEW STRENGTHS. I HAD ALSO UNCOVERED OLD ONES THAT I HAD SUPPRESSED BECAUSE I DIDN'T THINK I WAS WORTHY OF THEM. OUR CHOICES CARRY

INTENT WITH THEM, AND THAT IS PROBABLY OUR BIGGEST POWER. IF THERE IS A FIELD OF ENERGY THAT CONNECTS US WITH NATURE, GOD, AND THE UNIVERSE, IT MUST BE FUELED BY INTENT.

NO MATTER WHAT MAJOR OR MINOR DECISIONS YOU MAKE DURING THE DAY, YOU AFFECT YOUR OWN PATH AND THOSE OF OTHERS AROUND YOU. THE STRONGER THE INTENT, THE MORE POWER THE ACTION TAKES ON. WE CAN BECOME POWERFUL BEYOND IMAGINATION WHEN WE PUT OUR MINDS TO IT.

MY DAD USED TO SAY TO ME AS A CHILD, "KEITH, YOU CAN DO ANYTHING IF YOU MAKE UP YOUR MIND TO DO IT." HOW WISE THOSE WORDS WERE, BUT WE OFTEN DON'T LEARN THOSE CHILDHOOD LESSONS UNTIL LATER IN LIFE.

WE CAN ENERGIZE OURSELVES INTO ACTION AND SPUR ON THE PEOPLE AROUND US TO ACT AS WELL. TAKE NELSON MANDELA, FOR EXAMPLE. FROM HIS INSIGHTS, DETERMINATION, AND SELF-SACRIFICE, HE UNITED A PEOPLE AND CHANGED HIS COUNTRY FOREVER. HE CHOSE TO FOLLOW A RISKY PATH, AND HE FILLED IT WITH THE INTENT OF BETTERING THE LIVES OF

MILLIONS OF PEOPLE. THE RESULTS SPEAK FOR
THEMSELVES.

BEING A BABY-BOOMER, THE ERA OF PRESIDENT
JOHN F. KENNEDY WAS INSPIRING WHEN HE GOT
THE NATION TO FOCUS ON PUTTING A MAN ON
THE MOON. AN IMMENSE AMOUNT OF EFFORT
ACCOMPLISHED SO MUCH IN SUCH A SHORT
TIME, AND THE COUNTRY WAS ENERGIZED BY HIS
LARGER THAN LIFE GOAL.

As I sat on the bank of the slow-moving river, I could listen to the birds and monkeys in the trees. Off in the distance, I could see an elephant being ridden by its handler. As they crossed the river, they were silhouetted against the setting sun and the stream of orange light reflecting off the water. A long, narrow, carved canoe with two men standing up paddling crossed just downstream. They carried a load of two individuals on their way home, standing next to bicycles.

I sipped my chai, took a deep breath, and absorbed the moment, thankful for my choices. I'd made some great ones, and I'd made some lousy ones. Each had added zest to my life, and wasn't that what it was all about? A life without zest is one that has been wasted. It's all a matter of choice. Difficult lives can still be full of excitement if one chooses to look at it that way. Upon returning to my room, I unpacked some clothes, cleaned up in my little bungalow, and then ate dinner with Phalad. He took the time to share with me what I'd be doing the next day. The day would start with a canoe ride downriver in the early morning and then a walk through the jungle, we would return to the camp midday. After that, I would take an elephant ride for several hours to look for rhino and other wildlife.

It felt good to climb into my sleeping bag and listen to the birds of the night in Chitwan. I had once again packed a lot into a day, and I was so grateful for my fortunate life. I was exhausted and asleep in no time.

RIVERS, ELEPHANTS, AND RHINOS

The alarm on my watch went off. I opened my eyes to the natural light in my bungalow, which had an eerie glow to it. I knew instantly that we were blanketed in fog. How could I get so lucky to be in a natural fog two days in the same week? I was so hard to please. The air was cool and refreshing, and I couldn't wait to meet Godi to start my day.

A few minutes later, Godi came just as promised, and he took me for a walk to see the birds of the area near the elephant holding area. The elephants really captured my attention and, consequently, several rolls of film. Their massive gray bodies, shrouded in the morning fog, made for great photography subjects, and when I got home, I was very pleased with the pictures. Intermingled with the elephants were small fires that were built by the handlers for warmth and cooking. Through the fog, I could see the dark elephants rocking back and forth, tugging against the heavy metal chains attached to one hind leg. The chain was connected to eight-foot by twelve-inch wood posts sunk deep in the ground. The odd mixture of odors of dung, the damp earth, the smoke from the fires, and the fog literally hung in the air.

Some of the elephants were a joy to be with, while others were outright mean; given the treatment some of them received, I couldn't blame them. They swayed their large trunks back and forth with sad eyes that followed me as I walked by. The elephants would trumpet as they were mounted and whacked on the head with a stick, which told them to move out into the jungle for a day's work. Having a great love for all animals, I couldn't help but feel sorry for the giant creatures. Their demeanor was that of docile and loving animals; they were so ill-treated that they expressed rebellion with sounds of dismay. It tugged at my heart to witness their anguish.

Mankind can be so cruel in the name of work and profits. I've never been much of a Greenpeace promoter, but witnessing this mistreatment almost made me want to join and boycott somebody. I realize that we humans have used animals to do our work for centuries, but why can't it be done with compassion and understanding of the workload that any animal carries? Decent treatment would go a long way to help the animals endure and work in a healthy environment, rather than one where they die early due to poor treatment, food, and medical attention.

The fog was denser on the river than it was around the camp, and I could barely see as I climbed into one of the carved long boats. They were about thirty feet long and only eighteen to twenty-four inches wide at the broadest point.

We were an international group again today; I could hear Polish, German, and English being spoken through the fog. It was a wonderful experience to float along quietly this way. I was sure that the men paddling had made this trip a thousand times and could tell where we were, but for me, it was really cool not knowing where I was and only sensing the jungle along the bank. It was very quiet except for the sounds of the water and the birds high up in the trees. When I looked at my watch, it was 6:30 a.m., the sunrise was occurring, and the fog hadn't burned off. The air was filled with the fragrance of the water, the reeds along the bank, and my canoe with its musty, old, wet, wood scent.

There was a paddler in the front of the boat and one at the rear, and they shouted from one boat to another in the fog. I supposed they wanted to keep together and were probably trying to make sure they pulled ashore at the same place. They all smoked terrible smelling cigarettes, and the stench of the burning tobacco burned my nose. I could remember when I smoked how much I loved the smell of a freshly lit cigarette. I think American tobacco does have an initially intriguing fragrance, but after American cigarettes have been burning for a few minutes, they smell bad too. Asian tobacco is of such poor quality, and the paper is not the best, so they smell awful. Just one man's opinion.

Toward the end of the canoe trip, the fog had begun to lift, and I could see the jungle on both sides of the river. The water was very smooth, almost like glass, and I could see the two other canoes twenty or so feet on either side of us. We tourists, being tourists, waved to each other, smiling as if we'd found a long-lost friend. We acted like kids. Everyone seemed fascinated with the tranquil experience. We'd been on the water for almost an hour when the guides brought the long boats to the left bank. The front paddlers pulled the canoes slightly onto the bank so we could get out, and then they pushed them back into the water. The men turned the boats upstream, laughing and talking to each other as they paddled. They seemed to have a pleasant job, which they were enjoying.

Our little band of people, all dressed in hiking boots, shorts, and light jackets, split up and walked off in different directions with our separate guides. Godi and I talked in low tones so as not to frighten off any animals. Over the next few hours, we spotted wild turkeys, colorful chickens, black monkeys, and a few monkeys that were pure white.

Godi whispered to be quiet, so we walked up stealthily and slowly upon some spotted deer. They were tan with white spots on their hindquarters and about half the size of the mule deer in Colorado. We sat still and watched them for a few minutes until suddenly, their heads shot up almost in unison; their noses twitched, smelling the air. They had caught our scent and quickly ran off in the opposite direction. I was amazed by their swiftness and beauty as they leaped into the brush and out of sight.

––––––––––

TWO COMPONENTS SEEM TO SURROUND EVERYTHING WE DO—CLARITY AND INTENT. IF YOU COULD SEE THE PROBLEM CLEARLY IN YOUR HEAD, AND ONLY HAD THE INTENT TO SOLVE IT WITHOUT BEING TIED TO A SPECIFIC OUTCOME, A SOLUTION WOULDN'T ELUDE YOU. BE TOO CLOSE TO THE DESIRED OUTCOME, AND YOU WILL WAIT UNTIL THE COWS COME HOME FOR A SOLUTION. MAN, DO I HAVE A PROBLEM WITH THAT ONE. I ALWAYS HAVE A SET OUTCOME THAT I'D LIKE TO SEE. I THINK MOST PEOPLE DO, AND IT'S A HABIT THAT'S DIFFICULT TO BREAK. IN THE WESTERN WORLD, WE ARE TAUGHT TO SET GOALS AND FOLLOW THEM THROUGH TO COMPLETION. IN THE SALES GAME, WHICH I WORKED IN FOR

OVER TWENTY YEARS, THOSE GOALS NEED TO BE ACCOMPLISHED FOR BONUSES, TRIPS, AND THE APPRECIATION OF THE SALES MANAGER.

THOSE PHILOSOPHIES CARRY OVER INTO YOUR PERSONAL LIFE, SO YOU EXPECT THE SAME SATISFACTION WITH OUTCOMES REALIZED. ANYONE WHO HAS BEEN IN ANY KIND OF PERSONAL RELATIONSHIP CAN ATTEST THAT WHEN YOU ADD ANOTHER INDIVIDUAL TO THE MIX, THOSE OUTCOMES CAN VARY A GREAT DEAL.

SUDDENLY, YOU HAVE A CONFLICT TO DEAL WITH THAT'S VERY DIFFERENT FROM THOSE AT WORK. YOU CAN EXPECT CERTAIN GOALS TO BE MET IN THE WORKPLACE, BUT IN YOUR PERSONAL LIFE, YOU MUST LEARN TO LET GO.

LEARNING WHAT ISSUES ARE IMPORTANT ENOUGH TO TURN OVER TO GOD IS A LESSON IN AND OF ITSELF. YOU DON'T WANT TO BE INDISCRIMINATE AND JUST GIVE GOD ALL YOUR PROBLEMS. YOU MUST TRY TO SOLVE A GREAT MANY ON YOUR OWN. THEN THE QUESTION ARISES: WHAT'S IMPORTANT AND WHAT'S NOT? MOST OF US LEARN COMMON SENSE WHEN WE ARE GROWING UP, SO START WITH THAT.

USING YOUR "COMMON SENSE" MEANS YOU DO
SOMETHING THAT ISN'T OUT OF THE ORDINARY
BUT IS COMMONLY UNDERSTOOD. DON'T LET
FEAR KEEP YOU FROM SOLVING A PROBLEM
BY YOURSELF BECAUSE YOU WILL FEEL MUCH
BETTER ABOUT YOURSELF IF YOU DO SOLVE IT. IF
COMMON SENSE SAYS YOU NEED HELP, THEN BY
ALL MEANS, ASK FOR IT, WITH SINCERITY
AND INTENT.

───────────

All along the way, we found rhino droppings; actually, we smelled them first—whew! I know this is gross, but you wouldn't believe how big the droppings were. They were shaped like a cow patty, but four inches thick and eighteen inches wide. No, I didn't measure them; I just guessed. I didn't want to get any closer than I had too. You sure wouldn't want to step in one—you might disappear!

Off in the jungle, we could hear the rhino, but Godi said we didn't want to get too close to them since they were often danger-ous. Later, back at camp, I heard the Poles came very close, and they were indeed frightened by the huge, gray creatures. On the walk back to camp, we came across several elephants grazing next to the trail. They left us alone, but I got a lot of photos.

The blisters on my feet hadn't completely healed, so I was wear-ing my tennis shoes They didn't give me the support I would have liked, but I was not carrying any equipment or a pack, which my feet liked a lot better, especially the big toe with the stitches. Not being in any hurry, Godi and I took our time. He pointed out a lot of wildlife as we got to know each other. Four hours later, we came to the river directly across from our camp and boarded a boat for the short trip to the other side.

My little safari village or camp was a collection of one-bedroom bungalows. Each had a bathroom with a cold-water shower. They were built out of bamboo with thatched roofs. Rock-lined dirt paths led to each bungalow from the main building where we ate, toward the road to town, and to the river. The many tall, tropical trees and small shrubberies all around the village made it feel luxurious.

I ate lunch with Godi and then took a nap for an hour. The nice advantage of this part of my trip was that I was being taken care of and really didn't have to fend for myself at all. I found a bamboo chair and small table on the riverbank under a huge tree. I sat and wrote in my journal while watching the locals walk by.

I couldn't help but wonder, as I sat peacefully, whether it would be as easy to let go of my control over life and its daily problems when I returned home. Here, I had been able to turn them over to God and let God and my soul guide me and help with the difficulties I encountered. Out in the wilderness on my trek, it was a relief to accomplish letting go. When I returned home, with its chaotic lifestyle, I was not so sure I would be able to do it as easily. I knew it should be the same, but it seemed different somehow. In Nepal, I just said, "All right, God; it's yours to solve," and I'd let go of the problem. Almost, as if by magic, a solution would appear. Having faith and trust and learning to let go, could it really be that easy— no matter where you were, could it really be that easy? Is that the lesson? Could this be life's key? And does it apply to all situations or just certain ones?

As I sat and wrote, I also came to the realization of how much tenacity and resilience I had discovered in myself during my trek. It's not easy to accept our mistakes sometimes. I should have hired a guide and didn't. I had to learn from mistake and find my way out. Being lost gave me a chance to push through pain and fear and discover how strong I was. As I looked back on my life, these qualities were always there, but I didn't give them any credence. I knew I would be stronger when I returned to my normal life back home.

ANOTHER ESSENTIAL INGREDIENT TO LOWERING STRESS IS MAINTAINING A QUIET MIND. BEING IN NEPAL AND ALONE ALLOWED ME TO GAIN A REAL SENSE OF MYSELF THROUGH LEARNING HOW TO GET VERY QUIET WHEN IT COUNTS. BY OBTAINING THAT PEACEFUL STATE OF MIND WHEN I NEEDED TO, I COULD ALMOST PHYSICALLY FEEL A TOTAL RELEASE OF MY PROBLEMS. WESTERNERS SEEM TO BE MOVING AWAY FROM THIS CONCEPT, BUT ONE DAY WE WILL REGRET THE LOSS OF THIS ABILITY.

THE NEW SCIENCE CALLED QUANTUM PHYSICS HAS ENTERED THIS AREA IN A BIG WAY. CLASSICAL PHYSICS DEALT WITH ITEMS THAT TODAY ARE ONLY COMMON SENSE. THE QUANTUM THEORIES DEAL WITH PROBABILITIES, NOT CERTAINTIES. PHYSICS IS RAPIDLY BECOMING VERY PHILOSOPHICAL IN ITS APPROACH TO CONSCIOUSNESS AND THOUGHT. THE MANIFESTATION OF OUR THOUGHTS IS A PRODUCT OF THE POWER OF OUR MIND AND SOUL. WHEN THE PHONE RINGS AND YOU KNOW WHO IT IS, OR WHEN YOU AND A FRIEND HAVE THE SAME THOUGHT AND SAY IT OUT LOUD AT THE SAME TIME, THOSE ARE INDICATIONS OF

JUST HOW MUCH OUR THOUGHTS ARE IN SYNC
WITH THE WORLD AROUND US.

IN THE NEXT CENTURY, QUANTUM PHYSICS
WILL HELP US DISCOVER MANY THINGS, IT WILL
MAKE THE TWENTIETH CENTURY LOOK LIKE THE
MIDDLE AGES. I HOPE I LIVE LONG ENOUGH TO
SEE SOME OF IT COME TO PASS. WE LIVE IN THE
MOST EXCITING TIMES; DON'T YOU JUST LOVE IT?

As I sat in the warm afternoon sun, Godi brought me a chai, then left just as quietly as he arrived; I could have gotten used to this lifestyle very quickly. I watched the long boats silently moving up and down the wide, smooth river. Upstream, I could see an elephant crossing the river; his handler sat on the massive beast's shoulders, rocking back and forth, as the elephant walked gracefully through the muddy-colored water. I took a deep breath, closed my eyes, and sank immediately into a relaxed state of mind. I concentrated on listening to the sounds around me: the birds, the breeze, faint voices, the occasional barking dog, and the beating of my heart. If tension were a black liquid, I could envision it seeping out the bottoms of my feet and into the ground as I released it from my entire body. When you can fully release tension, the sensation of comfort in your body is astonishing.

Life is a process of learning who we are through our awareness. In this process, we work with life in a trial-and-error fashion. New experiences come our way, and we seek clarity about ourselves in those experiences—how we relate to them and where we fit it in. Using my meditation to release tension, to gain clarity of my intentions and to promote them, to ask God for guidance and learning, to trust and have faith in the process, is all part of the learning experience. Nothing in life comes just from desire; you must act to move up the ladder of awareness. Meditation is a way to act, albeit a very passive one, but maybe the most important.

After I had rested by the river, Godi reappeared and led me to the staging area for the elephant safari. I don't know about other places, but here, to mount an elephant, an eight-foot-tall platform had been built. I climbed up and then stepped across onto the back of the elephant where I sat on a big pillow that was on sort of a wooden saddle.

One of the goals of the ride was to find rhino and any other wildlife. Sitting high and looking over the grass and bushes, we could see all sorts of deer, birds, and monkeys.

Suddenly, as we broke out into a clearing, seven adult rhinos and a baby were visible. Other than at a zoo, I had never been very close to a rhino; I was amazed by their size and speed. Even the baby could really run when it was trying to keep up with its mom. We followed them for a while, and I was astounded by the sound made collectively by the hooves of the rhino and elephants. It would be akin to that of a herd of buffalo on the prairie. The gray armor-like skins on the rhino gleamed in the afternoon sun as they slowed and meandered through the underbrush eating plants. For such huge animals, they were swift and agile. When they got tired of us, they galloped off toward the river.

It was a beautiful afternoon without a cloud in the sky and balmy temperatures. Every so often, I saw so many colors that I felt like I was on sensory overload. The animals, flowers, trees, grasses, water, colorful birds, and the sky made for a variegated scene. I went through three rolls of film. Some of the pictures, sadly, were blurry because I was rocking back and forth on the elephant.

By the time I returned to my room, it was early evening, and I was beat. The wooden saddle had rubbed the backs of my legs raw, and I was tired from hanging on. I took a shower and a nap before dinner. Phalad invited me to have dinner with him and then go into the small local town to see a cultural dance. I had told him that I loved spicy food, so he prepared some outstanding Indian dishes for me. They were indeed hot, but after bland Nepalese food, I relished the new flavors.

We walked about a mile into town, and I found it a lot like Karkarvita, where I had begun my trek almost a month earlier—bustling with activity but hardly any tourists; just the way I liked it. The dust from the dirt streets and the light from the low wattage bulbs in the streetlights gave the scene a perpetual, soft haze.

Phalad led me to a square where a lot of local people had gathered. There, tiki torches were the only source of light, and they gave the square a festive feeling. Kids ran around giggling, dogs barked, and adults talked and laughed; this was a community affair. I found the experience of being with locals doing what they liked especially rewarding. It wasn't like traveling to a place where local people perform nightly cultural shows for the tourists. This was how they lived, without fanfare.

Sixteen men and boys entered the square, and everyone became quiet and then applauded. They were dressed in colorful, traditional Nepali clothing and began slowly banging the two wooden batons that they were holding. At first, they struck only their own, but then they incorporated a dance where they struck the other dancers' batons. Rotating, dancing, and chanting, the circle of dancers moved first clockwise and then turned to go counter-clockwise. The crowd clapped occasionally and called out to the dancers. They were obviously proud of their fathers, sons, and brothers and their dancing skills. I, too, was impressed by their accomplishment; they were well-trained and enjoyed what they were doing. They performed twice with an intermission in the middle.

Afterward, Phalad and I walked slowly back to the camp. Having been educated in Kathmandu, he spoke excellent English. He told me about his life, goals, desires, and hobbies. He saw his life as a grand adventure and held much hope for his future. I enjoyed talking with him, but I was tired and ready for bed. We said goodnight, and I was asleep in no time.

FINAL DAYS: REFLECTIONS AND LOOKING TO THE FUTURE

As I sat on the plane somewhere over the Pacific reminiscing about my last days in Nepal, my trip had already started to feel like a dream. Memories are like that, aren't they? Learning to live in the moment is so important because once that moment is gone, the reality of it is gone too. Although you may retain some images clearly, other sensations begin to alter and diminish in their intensity.

I had enjoyed my time with Godi and Phalad in Chitwan and was sad to leave. The days in the lowlands with them and the beautiful surroundings had allowed me time to recover from my arduous trek. Being close to the animals of that region had brought me a sense of real familiarity with a different kind of nature than I'd had in the high country. I spent most of that last day packing up and then riding in the car back to Kathmandu. Travel days are sometimes lost days, but I enjoyed returning to Kathmandu, watching the landscape change and the reappearance of the Himalayas.

The staff at the Pothala recognized me, greeted me warmly, and then settled me into a room with a single queen-sized bed. The weather in Kathmandu was cool and overcast. Many of the rooms in the hotel were empty because the tourists had headed to warmer climates and the trekkers had started their journeys. It was, after all, now December; the streets were much less crowded, and most people were dressed in warmer clothing.

While sitting in the courtyard at Narayan's, I met a girl named Gisele from Austria. She had been on the road for three months and was going to India in a couple of days. We talked easily for about an hour until she noticed she was beginning to have an upset stomach. She left to retrieve some medicine in her room and then do some errands, but we made plans to meet again in the late afternoon for coffee and maybe dinner.

I had some purchases to make for friends and family, so I left Narayan's shortly after that. When we did meet around four o'clock, Gisele was feeling worse and went to bed, saying we would meet for breakfast the next day.

I decided to begin work on this book, so I went to the Greek restaurant for moussaka and a beer. I felt like a veteran traveler as I sat and listened to a few people who had just arrived. They spoke of things I had spoken of when I first arrived in Nepal three years earlier, such as the uniqueness of the architecture, the poverty, the taxi drivers, the lack of English spoken, and their inability to understand the natives. They were excited to be here to experience a new culture and to see the Himalayas firsthand. I'm sure that the restaurant owners heard these conversations over and over.

My small wooden table had a candle and was next to a window so I could watch the people on the street. While I ate, I got a good outline started and felt a sense of accomplishment. I knew my daily journal would provide a good foundation since my memory would be fallible. After a while, I felt the need to get outdoors.

I walked the streets for a couple of hours, knowing this experience would all be a memory soon, so I didn't want to give up on it just yet. I walked past shops where I had purchased items, and the shopkeepers nodded to me. Maybe it was my pace, an air of understanding where I was, and the look of a weary traveler that made me appear different to the locals. They, too, appeared different to me, not as foreign, more as friends or at least acquaintances. I had been down most of the streets numerous times in my two visits, and a familiarity warmed my soul as I saw places and things that I cherished. I especially valued the small stupas with their offerings of marigolds strewn about, shops devoted just to trekkers and climbers' equipment, and the little restaurants smelling of chai, spices, and grease. It was getting dark, and I had nowhere to go; I returned to the Pothala. I wrote in my journal, read a book I had picked up at the bookstore frequented by travelers in need of some reading material, and fell asleep.

The next day, Gisele and I met for breakfast. She was feeling much better, so we made plans to meet in the hotel lobby at four o'clock and spend our last evening in Kathmandu together. I wanted to find some yak wool as a gift to my dad for his knitting, and I knew it would take some time to locate a vendor. I knew my mother would like a Kashmir wrap, and I knew where I would get it while I was out.

I took my camera along, knowing I would be in the back streets of Kathmandu. The unusual photo was just waiting to be taken. I must have walked six miles during the day since I found it difficult to locate the knitting wool. I shot almost three rolls of black and white film, having found many unusual photos needing to be taken.

I sat at a restaurant near Monkey Mountain and listened to the chanting of the monks in the monastery across the street. As I ate my dahl and rice, I found myself chanting the simple phrase too. I have no idea what it meant, but like most mantras, it was melodic and calming. The people in the restaurant smiled to me in an understanding way.

When I had finished, I climbed the steps to the monastery and took several photos of the young boys chanting. They were sitting on the floor, in two rows on each side of the temple facing each other. I was somewhat of a pleasant distraction to them. They all noticed me right away as I stepped into the entrance, so I ventured no further. I smiled and nodded to them; they kept chanting, but they smiled at me and then discreetly to each other. The temple smelled of incense and was very clean. The old wooden structure had seen many young monks come and go over the centuries, and yet it was warm, familiar, and friendly. I waved goodbye to the children, and they waved back, not missing a beat in their chant. Discipline at such early ages is impressive.

By the time I had finished with my shopping, it was one o'clock; I returned to my room for a nap and to clean up. At two-thirty, I went up on the roof, wrote in my journal, and just sat in the sun. I hated the idea that I was going home, but I was ready to return. I loved being on the road alone, and on this trip, I had discovered so much about myself and the world around me.

Gisele found out from the front desk clerk that I was on the roof. She joined me there at four o'clock. We wanted something to drink and stopping at the only store that sold liquor, we bought a pint of Indian whiskey. It turned out to be smooth stuff as whiskeys go. I'm not much of a drinker, but I had to admit it tasted pretty good. We went to the vegetarian restaurant up the street, ordered Cokes, and sat and talked for a couple of hours. When we got hungry, we went to a local Indian restaurant and had dinner.

Gisele was involved with a man in Austria, but she had felt

the need to travel and see the world for a while before making up her mind about a serious, long-term relationship with him. I was impressed with the maturity of her actions. At thirty-one, she was level-headed and sincere. To some people, a long-term relationship sounds great, but the willingness to compromise and stay committed needs to be understood. This was Gisele's way to gain insight into her own soul and discover what she really wanted.

During our discussions, I examined how I had jumped into relationships throughout my life without enough forethought, and I vowed to follow her example in the future. In the two days since I had first met Gisele, we had become close and shared personal intimacies openly. It was nice to be with someone you could share things with and know you wouldn't be judged.

We returned to her room, lit some incense, and lay on her bed like spoons, just holding each other until 2:00 a.m., when I left. Two travelers meeting in a strange land sharing their lives and warmth with each other without getting physical was a fascinating experience and one I'll always treasure. Since Gisele was to leave the next day at noon for India and me on the following day for Bangkok, it made our time together special.

On my last full day, I saw Gisele off and then just wandered the streets of Thamel, Kathmandu, Patan, and Monkey Mountain until I was tired. Then I returned to the Pothala to sit on the roof and write. My writing had begun to take over as my means of expression, and I did enjoy it so. It was a beautiful day, with clear blue skies and a cool westerly breeze. I was beginning to have a sense of closure, and I supposed that was good.

It would be so nice to get home and find my first book well on its way to being successful. Whether or not it was didn't really matter as I now had a new plan to retire from insurance and make my living writing, speaking, traveling, and doing photography. I hoped I could find a way to make all of that happen. Maybe it was already being set up for me, and I didn't even know it yet. *Is that my future,*

I wondered, *to be able totally to release and detach, and have the best happen?* I thought so.

I rested and read the afternoon away, had a good dinner at the vegetarian restaurant, and went back to my room to finish packing. I slept well; completely relaxed.

The next morning, I had my last breakfast at Narayan's and wrote in my journal before Lava was to give me a ride to the airport. I'd discovered just how much I missed my family and friends and how much I truly cared for them. As I wrote in my journal, I realized that I looked forward to seeing everyone soon. Although I loved being on the road, there still was no place like home. Later in the day, I had an uneventful flight to Bangkok, where I got an in-airport hotel room, watched a movie, and went to sleep. The excitement I experienced going in the other direction a month earlier had settled into just the love of travel and doing it with ease.

I flew to Seoul, South Korea, and now was mid-Pacific on the way to Los Angeles. It sure took a long time to get home with all of those stops, but then, I was 12,000 miles from home, so it wasn't going to go by quickly.

TWENTY-TWO YEARS LATER

The manuscript for "Tenacity" sat on the shelf for over twenty years. When I got home from Nepal in '95, I spent much of the next year transcribing my journal notes into one document. It went through many iterations and was almost completely lost several times with computer crashes.

I approached several local publishers and didn't get any interest. Mailed it to a few more and logged nothing but rejection letters. My insurance practice continued to flourish and took most of my time, and after a while, I forgot about it.

Many years later a friend of mine from Toastmasters invited me to speak to her marketing group and to tell my Nepal story.

Although I didn't feel ready to speak publicly, I relented, and on a cold, snowy Colorado morning I delivered my first talk. Unexpectedly, when I finished, I was energized and ready for more. I began developing a keynote speech and looking for places to deliver it and practice. Over a couple of years, I gave my speech over seventy times and joined the National Speakers Association as a professional member.

Learning from other professional members, I found out that to attract speaking business I needed a book, a website, Facebook page, Twitter page, business email address, and a multitude of other things. Remembering what I'd written many years earlier, I went to the basement and dug through a lot of three-ring binders to find the last edition of my manuscript. Finally, I found what appeared to be the last one I worked on, dusted it off, and went through months of editing and re-editing until it was ready for a professional editor. The manuscript went through four editors, all of whom gave me different advice and changes. Hopefully, you've enjoyed this final iteration.

During the past twenty-odd years, I was aware when certain things I had written about in my Nepal journal were coming to fruition and when others were falling by the wayside. My journal was full of ideas, aspirations, and dreams that I hoped would come true; some have, some haven't yet.

Retiring early from my insurance practice was a goal I had decided on while I was lost and I achieved that in 2002 at age 55. However, I got bored quickly and went back to college to study philosophy and creative writing. I had studied and read a lot during the previous decade, but it had been mostly new age philosophers. At the college level, I went back to the Greeks, Romans, Phoenicians, and others. I got to know the ancients up close and personal. What an adventure they provided along with a whole new level of excitement.

The relationship I longed for disappeared for good, but it had produced my son Michael who surfaced into my life when he was sixteen.

Today, as I look back on my trip, a couple of things come to mind. If you truly believe in something and in your ability to accomplish it—you will. Tenacity, resilience, imagination and purpose are the qualities that make it happen, and they became the cornerstone of my speaking. This trip was meant to be a growth experience for me, and I knew it going in. That belief made it happen without major mishap. I wanted an adventure, and I was willing to open myself up to receive it. I also had a sense of *knowing* that I would be taken care of if I would allow it, and not force things to happen my way.

Secondly, I discovered that there is a definite difference between knowing a path and walking the path. Back home, I knew my path and was trying to follow it, but I wasn't succeeding very well. After my trek, I was walking the path, and I knew it. My heart was open to the powers of the universe, and I was humble enough to realize that those are the only powers that count anyway. I can be the person I choose to be, walk a path in line with my intentions, and eliminate expectations.

Learning to let go and listen, having faith, and trusting the loving universe to take care of you are key if you are to follow through and take appropriate action. There is a whole new world out there just waiting for you to discover it, but the desire must exist in your heart first. Take time to find it, and you will love the results. Pay attention to your growth, and above all else, have faith in the process. Namaste'.

Book Keith to Speak Today:
Office: 303-973-1643
Cell: 303-888-7694
keith@keithrenninson.com
www.KeithRenninson.com

Connect with Keith Online:
Facebook.com/Keith-Renninson
Twitter.com/RenninsonKeith
Linkedin.com/in/keithrenninson
Tenacitythebook.com

ABOUT THE AUTHOR

Keith Renninson is a Colorado native and Vietnam Army veteran whose favorite phrase is, "Everything you desire is just outside your comfort zone." Now retired after forty-plus years in the insurance/financial planning world, he is speaking and writing full-time on the many experiences he has enjoyed while traveling the world. He has had an adventurous life as a racecar driver, mountain climber, actor, voice-over talent in radio commercials, bicycle racer, skier, and trekker to remote locations.

Keith's first award-winning book was *The Pain & Joy of Love: A collection of poetry, short stories, and black and white photography.* That was followed by a multi-authored book, *101 Ways to Improve Your Life*. In 2005, working with co-author Mike Kelly, Keith helped produce an illustrated children's book, *Zooch the Pooch, My Best Friend,* designed to assist children through the process of grief.

As a Professional Member of the National Speakers Association, Keith speeches cover topics such as tenacity, understanding, resilience, purpose, focus, problem-solving, innovation, creativity, imagination, brainstorming techniques, relating to stress management in the workplace. Keith's workshop: ***Making your journey through life a total adventure…Let's take a "TRIP"*** (Tenacity, Resilience, Imagination and Purpose) is designed for business leaders, employees and entrepreneurs of all kinds.

www.ingramcontent.com/pod-product-compliance
Lightning Source LLC
Chambersburg PA
CBHW021227090426
42740CB00006B/419